LIFE
—AT—
WARP
SPEED

THE TRAVELER'S GUIDE TO

LIFE
—AT—
WARP
SPEED

30 SHORT READINGS
TO HELP YOU SLOW DOWN
AND CATCH UP WITH GOD

FRITZ RIDENOUR

AUTHOR OF THE BESTSELLING HOW TO BE A CHRISTIAN WITHOUT BEING RELIGIOUS

Regal Books
A Division of Gospel Light
Ventura, California, U.S.A.

Published by Regal Books
A Division of GL Publications
Ventura, California 93006
Printed in U.S.A.

Library of Congress Cataloging-in-Publication Data
Ridenour, Fritz.
       The traveler's guide to— life at warp speed : 30 short readings to help you slow down and catch up with God / Fritz Ridenour.
       p.   cm.
       Includes bibliographical references.
       ISBN 0-8307-1357-3
       1. Meditations.   I. Title.
BV4832.2.R525   1990
242—dc20   90-38261
                                                                          CIP

Any omission of credits is unintentional. The publisher requests documentation for future printings.

Rights for publishing this book in other languages are contracted by Gospel Literature International (GLINT) foundation. GLINT also provides technical help for the adaptation, translation, and publishing of Bible study resources and books in scores of languages worldwide. For further information, contact GLINT, Post Office Box 488, Rosemead, California, 91770, U.S.A., or the publisher.

TO
Dr. Milford Sholund
whose views of time and eternity
have always helped me deal with that nemesis called
The Deadline

Contents

How Can I Slow Down When I'm Moving So Fast?

If you're like a lot of people I talked to while researching this book, the thought of slowing down or cutting back is more than just slightly appealing. Oh, for even a few delicious hours of kicking back, going for a long walk, reading that book (*pile* of books?), praying, thinking or just "being," with no particular goal or deadline.

Alas, to most of us "slowing down" is a fantasy, a dream not to be realized in the immediate or even the distant future. There are kids to care for, bills to pay, clients or bosses to pacify, lawns to mow, shopping to do, Sunday School lessons to teach, meals to prepare, freeways to fight—life goes on and on...and on some more.

So, how do we "slow down" at all?

This book is a thirty-part "experiment" in giving you some ideas about how to begin. It is not a treatise on time management or a primer on how to be a success and still be spiritual. It is a gathering of some thoughts about how to slow down the inner pace of your life in order to "catch up with God." That may sound like a contradiction, but I prefer to call it a paradox.

As we head into the '90s, we are running faster than ever, trying to do it all and have it all, or at least avoid being run down from behind. We dash through life, and our daily routine seems to allow no time for God. At best, we pencil Him into our already crowded appointment books and to-do lists. We think we are moving so fast we've left the Lord behind in that sitting room that was so well described by Robert Munger in his classic little booklet, *My Heart Christ's Home.*

In truth, of course, God is never left behind. In fact, He is far ahead of us. The only way we will ever catch up is to slow down and focus on the "one thing" that is really necessary.

To focus on this one thing is not simply a matter of setting aside twenty more minutes for devotions. Logging more quiet time will undoubtedly help, but what is really needed is a quietness in our souls, which can only be found through what Henri Nouwen calls "moving our hearts to the center," where all other things fall into place.[1]

Getting to "The Center" is what this collection of brief essays tries to do. Some of the material may be quite familiar. But don't think getting to The Center—and staying there—is easy. What is easy is to be trapped at the outer edges of what God has for us—on the periphery of life in His kingdom, running the rat race instead of the race Jesus has marked out for us.

The "rat race" is a familiar term to those of my generation, which preceded the baby boomers, who were born between the late '40s and early '60s. To gather insights and ideas for this book, I interviewed men and women from both generations to see if they thought they were caught in the rat race. Some admitted they were, at least part of the time. Others (usually those twenty and thirty something) thought the rat race to be an anachronism left over from the '50s. To them the rat race suggested mindless repetition, hurrying blindly, not getting anywhere, going around and around, locked in like a gerbil on a wheel.

To describe their pace of living, the baby boomer generation related better to terms like "fast lane," "upwardly mobile," or "faster than a speeding bullet," as a hairdresser in her thirties put it. Above all, they at least wanted some direction for all their busy-ness and hurrying, a target for their lives, as hectic as they might be.

With all these opinions in mind, I have chosen to risk the occasional use of the term "rat race" to describe the kind of mindless rushing that leaves us frustrated and stressed out, wondering how we could stop the world for just a minute or two to get on the right track.

"Stressed out" has become a familiar part of our vocabulary in the last decade or two. Currently, most of society understands that stress—the wear and tear of daily life—can cause everything from headaches to hysterectomies, from nervous breakdowns to the unraveling of a marriage. I devote several chapters to coping with stress. Note I said "coping," because there is no way to avoid it. Indeed, the only people without stress reside in cemeteries.

I also devote several chapters to the rampant consumerism of our materialistic society where success is measured by how much we accumulate of that well-known commodity called Mammon. In our pursuit of money, possessions and prestige, we suffer from what one writer calls "affluenza."[2]

Jesus had much to say about materialism and He said most of it to the poor and middle-class folk, not the very rich. As uncomfortable as the label may sound, there is no way to deny that we live smack in the middle of the most materialistic culture in history. Materialism is not the only reason we get sucked into running the rat race, but it is surely a major one.

Ironically, the more we accumulate, the less time we have in our already crowded lives, because having, using, maintaining and preserving all this stuff takes precious minutes and hours. In the '80s, time became so precious that people were willing to pay $25 to $50 an hour to household service establishments for the simplest of services, like removing a light bulb broken off in the socket to delivering a package of hot dog buns to a family picnic.[3]

You may not have reached the point where you're hiring people to change your light bulbs, but you probably are feeling the time crunch enough to want some relief. You may be like the ox, which the poet describes as having no time to eat, plod, sleep, or even think.[4]

Above all, we need time to think and I pray that these brief chapters will help you get started. There are thirty readings in all. Some of them will, I hope, ring your bell and find somebody home. Others possibly may not say as much to your particular situation. This only suggests that everyone is on his or her own pilgrimage. Wherever we are or from whatever direction we're coming, we still need help with slowing down and taking time to figure out what it is we are really supposed to be doing besides smelling the daisies.

One nice thing about these chapters is that they are fairly short—designed to be read at the rate of one a day. I hope you will give this thirty-day experiment a try. Maybe, just maybe, among the deadlines, pressures, freeways and frustrations, you will find time to "slow down and catch up with God."

Notes
1. Henri J. M. Nouwen, *Making All Things New* (San Francisco: Harper and Row Publishers, 1981), pp. 42-43.
2. Randy Alcorn, *Money, Possessions and Eternity* (Wheaton: Tyndale House Publishers, Inc., 1989), p. 373.
3. See Nancy Gibbs, "How America Has Run Out of Time," *Time*, April 24, 1989, p. 67.
4. See Carmen Bernos de Gasztold, *Prayers from the Ark* (London: Macmillan Company, 1963), p. 55, "The Prayer of the Ox."

CHAPTER ONE

The Fast Lane Has No Speed Bumps

Ruth rode on my motor-bike
Directly in back of me;
I hit a bump at sixty-five
And rode on ruth-lessly.

Anonymous

"Be still, and know that
I am God."

Psalm 46:10 (*KJV*)

If you don't have much time to read this, I understand. According to *Time* magazine, we're smack in the middle of a "time famine"[1] and no one has any idea of when it will end. Who knows? Time may end first!

Meanwhile, life seems set on "fast lane" and we don't dare slow down. In the Los Angeles area, where I worked for many years, the freeways are a way of life for millions of commuters. Try driving even close to the speed limit in the fast lane and you are asking to be tailgated, or even run down. So, you move over to lane number two, where traffic flows a bit more sanely. Soon, however, another grill is in your bumper because some character has decided that whoever is in the fast lane is moving too slowly and now he wants to get around *you,* as well.

Dutifully, you pull into the slow lane where the pace seems much more reasonable. The trouble is, it's too reasonable. Now you're going just a little too slowly to make "good time," and so, after plugging along behind some truck for a few miles, you venture over into lane two and try your luck once more. After all, you have a schedule to keep and the slow lane just won't get you there on time.

Most of us claim we hate fast lane living. Oh, for a little more time in a quiet "parking place," where we could contemplate, read, pray or just sit. Unfortunately, we are more familiar with the typical routine of a lady named Lynn, who always finds herself in the fast lane, hurrying from one thing to another. In fact, she doesn't even need to leave the house. This morning the phone put her in the fast lane in a hurry when her husband, Kurt, called with the happy news that he was bringing a couple of clients home for dinner that evening, and could she do her usual magic thing with chicken and broccoli?

A few minutes later, it was Mr. Flannagan on the line saying, "Sorry to bother you on your day off, Lynn, but don't forget those expense reports we need typed. Just leave them on my desk first thing in the morning—thanks!"

Working part-time at home on your own computer has its pros and—with demanding bosses like Mr. Flannagan—its cons.

And now it's after lunch and we find Lynn in her familiar role as family cabbie—even though her mini-van is blue, not yellow. She has just dropped off several items for the church bulletin, wishing she could stop at the park nearby just to sit and take in God's handiwork, catch her breath and spend a few spare minutes in prayer. But, as usual, there are no spare minutes. She has to get her twelve-year-old soccer player to his game on time, as she fights afternoon gridlock to connect with her fifteen-year-old cheerleader who has just gotten out of a practice session.

"Can't you drive any faster, Mom?" wails her soccer player, also known as Tommy. "The game starts in ten minutes! If I'm late again, my coach is gonna bench me. You are staying to watch, aren't you?"

Two minutes later, part of Lynn's mission is accomplished...sort of. "Where *were* you, Mom?" inquires her cheerleader, whose name in real life is Jennifer. "I've been waiting here in front of the school for twenty minutes! How come you always pick everybody else up first? Did you forget about my algebra test? It's tomorrow, you know, and you promised you'd help me study tonight, remember? If I don't pass, I can't be a cheerleader. Can't *you drive any faster?*"

"I'm *driving* as fast as I *can!*" Lynn manages through gritted teeth, as she pulls up at her eighth red light in a row. Seven minutes to soccer game time and another fourteen blocks to the field. She'll never make it. Tommy will be benched, his self-esteem will shatter and he'll probably become a drug addict!

Then an intriguing thought blossoms in her mind: *Why not just let them both off here with bus fare* and drive off into the sunset? No one would blame you...*or would they?*

Lynn, by the way, is no figment of my imagination but one of several real live mothers I talked to not long ago. As she told the rest of us her tale of woe, I could make some pretty good guesses why she was in her present state. Undoubtedly she was a pleaser type who couldn't say no and really liked trying to cover all the bases to make everyone happy. But, like most pleasers, she falls a little further behind each day, and that afternoon when she hit that eighth red light in a row, it all had seemed too much.

Lynn would love to have more time to talk with friends, take that aerobics class or just linger over a cup of coffee. And then there's that continual longing to spend some time in prayer, thinking about God's Word and her relationship to Him. But her frantic pace makes it all seem hopeless. What was that old-fashioned term her dad often used while she was growing up? "Another day in the rat race," he'd often say.

"Well, it's still a rat race," Lynn sighs. "Only now we run it on freeways in the fast lane and call ourselves upwardly mobile." And then Lynn wonders, "Which lane would Jesus travel? Would He be roaring down the fast lane? Or would He even use the freeway?"

In his Gospel, Luke uses his reporter's eye to share a tiny scene during one of the Lord's busy days. Other players in this scene are Mary and Martha, two sisters who live in Bethany with their brother, Lazarus. Jesus is on His last swing through Palestine, headed for Jerusalem with His face "set like flint," fully knowing what lies ahead. But He stops at Bethany, a little less than two miles from Jerusalem's gates, to spend some time with His friends. Luke tells us what happened:

> As Jesus and his disciples were on their way, he came to a village where a woman named Martha opened her home to him. She had a sister called Mary, who sat at the Lord's feet listening to what he said. But Martha was distracted by all the preparations that had to be made. She came to Him and asked, "Lord, don't you care that my sister has left me to do the work by myself? Tell her to help me!"
>
> "Martha, Martha," the Lord answered, "you are worried and upset about many things, but only one thing is needed. Mary has chosen what is better, and it will not be taken away from her" (Luke 10:38-42).

This brief little drama has a lot to teach about fast lanes, slow lanes—and parking places. The rat race isn't a condition unique to the twentieth century. Back in the first century Martha came huffing and puffing up her own fast lane that day, thoroughly embroiled in a rat race of her own making. She was a hassled and harried hostess, trying to get dinner together, while the rest of them just sat out in the living room, talking and enjoying each other's company.

No wonder Martha got "distracted" or "encumbered." The biblical word actually means "pulled apart," and Martha was so anxious she actually started scolding Jesus for not sending Mary out to the kitchen to help!

Instead of getting irritated, Jesus said fondly, "Martha, Martha, you are worried and upset about many things, but only one thing is needed."

What did Jesus mean by "one thing"? It's possible that all He meant was that Martha had prepared too big a menu. She had too many dishes in the oven and had gotten herself into a terrible bind when all she needed to do was fix a few sandwiches.

But it's my guess Jesus meant more than that. Other-

The fast lane is a state of mind, not a certain ribbon of concrete between home and work.

---

wise, why did He tell Martha that Mary had chosen "what is better"?

The better part Mary chose was time with Jesus— enjoying Him and His teaching. Troubled by many things, Martha was missing the most important one. Was Jesus putting her down? It's true He was gently rebuking her, but He certainly wasn't criticizing being active, busy or hospitable. It's just that Martha's timing was a little off and her priorities were out of tune.

It wasn't that Martha's way of serving the Lord was bad, it was just that, *especially in this situation*, Mary's way was better. The Lord had traveled far and was almost at the end of His final journey to Jerusalem. He knew well what lay ahead—betrayal, a trumped up trial, a Cross. He wasn't concerned about eating a sumptuous seven-course meal; He simply wanted to fellowship with those He loved.

In these days of "time famines" and "time crunches," what does this little story have to teach us? In trying to show Jesus how much she loved Him, Martha had managed to jump into the fast lane and roar right by the parking place He had chosen. We need to go back and look again at Jesus' words, "Mary has chosen what is better." If we can choose that better way, everything else falls in place.

Henri Nouwen (*Making All Things New*) believes Jesus isn't saying we should forget about our responsibilities and live happily ever after, ignoring the schedules and activities that make up our daily lives. Jesus' response to the rat race is different. He wants us to center our attention on something else that is much more important. Instead of being frustrated by too many items on our to-do lists, He asks that we focus on "one necessary thing." He isn't asking us to leave the world but to live in it with a new sense of priorities: "Jesus does not speak about a change of activities, a change in contacts, or even a change of pace. He speaks about a change of heart."[2]

The rest of this book explores what it means to have a true "change of heart." Does it mean getting up an hour earlier in the morning to be sure to have devotions? Working fewer hours? Taking a time management course? All those ideas are good ones, but the change of heart that Nouwen speaks of goes deeper than that.

The fast lane is a state of mind, not a certain ribbon of concrete between home and work. If we want to choose "the better part," we need to start by following Jesus around and see where He goes and what He means.

Lord, help me choose the better part—focusing on You and letting other things fall into place as You see fit.

Are you a Martha? A Mary? Somewhere in between? Are you controlling your schedule, or does it control you?

What three steps can you take to turn things around and choose the better part?

Notes
1. See Nancy Gibbs, "How America Has Run Out of Time," *Time*, April 24, 1989, p. 58.
2. Henri J. M. Nouwen, *Making All Things New* (San Francisco: Harper and Row Publishers, 1981), pp. 41,42.

CHAPTER TWO

Burn On or Burn Out?

Someday I shall burst my buds
of calm...and blossom into
HYSTERIA.[1]

"The Lord is my shepherd; I shall
not want."

—Psalm 23:1 *(KJV)*

As we plunge pell-mell into the 1990s, terms like "burnout" and "stress attack" are common expressions. Just existing in the fast-lane society seems to keep most people under stress. Take a fellow named Frank, who has just escaped his stuffy, confining office at the end of a long, frustrating day, plagued by endless meetings and appointments, none of which have resolved or accomplished anything.

Inching up the freeway through 6:00 P.M. gridlock, Frank wonders how Mary is doing during her daily "piranha hour" when the kids swarm around her feet just before dinner, wanting everything, but doing nothing to help. Tonight is AWANA night, and Mary not only has to get the kids fed, but all of her materials ready, as well. It's a great program—the kids love it—but he wonders how Mary can handle being an AWANA leader and working part-time at the bank, too.

"Somebody's got to do it," Mary said when Frank asked her if she weren't biting off a little too much. "Besides, I like working in AWANA—something to *do* besides sitting and soaking every Sunday morning."

"Sitting and soaking" on Sunday mornings is about all Frank has time for at church these days. When the promotion came through, it meant longer hours and dropping the Sunday School class he had taught for more than a year.

"Hope they leave me something in the oven," Frank mutters as he slips into the fast lane in hopes of making better time. The trouble is, the fast lane is moving like all the others—at fifteen miles an hour. He wonders if he'll have time to do that report that's due on the boss's desk at 8:00 in the morning. Frank squirms uncomfortably as he remembers something the pastor had said in last Sunday's sermon, something about Jesus always making prayer a priority and how, when the pace of life around Him speeded up, Jesus always slowed down.

"But Jesus didn't have to deal with my problems," Frank groans. "If this thing doesn't speed up, I'll never make it, I'll never get home on time to get all my work done. There is always so much to do. I've got to talk to Mary about how we can both slow down."

However you want to describe Frank, he is under stress, a term introduced to everyday vocabularies back in the 1950s by Dr. Hans Selye of the Institute of Experimental Medicine and Surgery at the University of Montreal.[2] According to Dr. Selye, stress is the simple wear and tear caused by life's happenings, which may be pleasant or unpleasant. A lot of what you see and hear today about stress gives the impression that all stress is bad and should be avoided. But the truth is, just being alive puts you under stress. There is only one place where people have no stress—the cemetery. As one exhausted lady put it: "Life is so hard—it's just breathe, breathe, breathe, all the time!"

That's why doing things that are pleasant, productive or just plain fun can wear you out. Having a good day at work, being in a committee meeting where something actually gets done, or watching Johnny's Little League team win by one run in the last of the ninth—any of these things is stressful.

In Dr. Selye's terms, these positive sources of stress are known as "eustress," while negative stress—the bad stuff that wears you down—is called "distress." To measure the effects of positive or negative stress on the human body, one pair of researchers—Thomas Holmes and Richard Rahe—developed a Social Readjustment Rating Scale, which assigns Life Change Units to typical events that happen to most or many of us at one time or another.

Their list includes traumas like the death of a spouse (100 LCU's) to something as ordinary as moving (20 LCU's). The Holmes/Rahe Scale enables you to measure the amount of stress you've been under over the past twelve months. If it totals over 300 LCU's, you could be in danger of serious illness or other problems.

One of the devil's basic strategies is to get you so focused on your own frustrations that you forget to call on the One who knows exactly what you're going through.

The distress Frank encounters during freeway rush hour is definitely adding to his LCU total. And, ironically, being a follower of Christ doesn't seem to give him any magic power to deal with his fifteen-mile-an-hour pace as he tries to get home, grab a quick bite of dinner, and work several more hours to get the report done that is due in the morning.

In fact, recalling a sermon he heard just last Sunday turns his freeway battle into a guilt trip. Jesus may have slowed down when life speeded up, but Frank can't, or at least he thinks he can't. If Frank wanted to be honest, he'd tell you Jesus never had to drive clogged freeways for an hour a day each way. Jesus never had a wife, three kids under the age of seven, and a variable rate mortgage that has just varied upward.

As Frank creeps up the freeway, anxiety and frustration seem to push Jesus and His teachings further and further into the irrelevant background. Forgetting that power to cope with the stress of fighting freeways and too much work is only a prayer away, Frank slips deeper into the grip of distress.

I've been there with Frank a time or two, and perhaps you have, too. One of the devil's basic strategies is to get you so focused on your own frustrations that you forget to call on the One who knows exactly what you're going through, because He was "stressed at all points just as you are" (see Heb. 4:15).

The Gospel accounts show that Jesus' life was never relaxed for very long. When He did try to slip off for some quiet moments alone or to retreat with His disciples, the crowds came running after Him. The first chapter of Mark chronicles a typical day in Jesus' life when His popularity was at its highest point. He arrives in Capernaum and is invited to teach in the local synagogue, where He amazes the people by teaching out of personal authority, instead of just quoting the experts.

Suddenly, His teaching session becomes more than a little stressful when a man with an evil spirit jumps up and starts screaming. Hardly missing a beat, Jesus orders the evil spirit out of the man and continues teaching. Later He leaves the synagogue, goes to the home of Simon Peter and his brother, Andrew, and finds Simon's mother-in-law ill with a high fever. He heals her and then, for the rest of the day and far into the evening, He continues to heal people who are sick or demon-possessed.

That night He catches a little sleep, but very early the next morning—probably around 3:00 or 4:00 A.M.—Jesus gets up and goes off alone to pray. Simon and the others awake, find Jesus missing and go after Him. Coming upon Him at prayer, their first words are not "Good morning," or "Did you sleep well?" Instead, they greet

Him with, "Everyone is looking for you!" Apparently, the crowds were already starting to come back, and Jesus would soon be caught up in another stressful day of teaching and healing (see Mark 1:21-39).

What kept Jesus going? The "clue" to how He handled stress is obvious: repeatedly in the Gospel accounts we see Him slipping away alone to spend time in prayer, communing with His heavenly Father and "recharging His batteries" for the next day's activities. After long days of healing the sick, He would "withdraw to lonely places to pray" (see Luke 5:12-16). Before He chose twelve of His disciples to be apostles, He "spent the night praying to God" (see Luke 6:12-16).

In the final year of Jesus' ministry, His popularity decreases as opposition mounts. On the night before the horrors of the Cross, Jesus retreats to the Mount of Olives where He gathers strength for the ordeal before Him, praying, "Father, if you are willing, take this cup from me; yet not my will, but yours be done" (Luke 22:42). An angel comes to strengthen Jesus, but He prays *even more earnestly*, and His sweat is like "drops of blood falling to the ground" (Luke 22:44).

The next day, Jesus faces stress we cannot begin to fathom. There is no rating on the Holmes/Rahe scale for crucifixion, much less the moment when He cries out, "My God, My God, why have you forsaken me?" The Father has turned His face from the Son, who has become sin in order to redeem the world, but even now Jesus deals with the pain and the suffering by trying to communicate as He submits to His Father's will.

In all these examples, we find a principle for handling stress in the 1990s, when freeways grow more crowded and super commuters traveling a hundred miles or more each way to work become commonplace. On the surface, the answer seems elementary: pray more and try to get away on retreats whenever you can. That may sound a little simplistic for someone like Frank who is caught in freeway gridlock with nowhere to go but a little crazy. Nonetheless, prayerlessness is what is cutting Frank off from God's help, trapping him in feelings of being overwhelmed and defeated.

In his excellent book, *Too Busy Not to Pray*, Bill Hybels observes that surprising numbers of people are willing to settle for prayerless lives. He writes: "Don't be one of them. Nobody has to live like that. *Prayer is the key to unlocking God's prevailing power in your life.*"[3]

Whenever Jesus modeled certain *actions* for His disciples, He also modeled certain *attitudes*. The attitude that leads to burnout says: "I'm busy but I can handle it...if you want something done, you have to do it yourself...who's going to do it if I don't?" A dozen other excuses all add up to, "I'm indispensable, indestructible, and independent. I don't need to bother God with the regular routine; I'll save that for the really heavy stuff, like 7.1 earthquakes, colon cancer or a four-way bypass."

On the other hand, there is, however, a different attitude that helps us burn on instead of burn out, no matter how many curves life may toss our way. How to develop that attitude is the subject of the next chapter.

Lord, forgive my times of prayerlessness. Help me remember Your example to slip away and communicate with my heavenly Father.

List some major sources of stress in your life. Are there any you can eliminate? Which ones do you need to pray about more often?

Notes
1. Author unknown. Observed on a bumper sticker.
2. Dr. Selye's first book was *The Stress of Life* (New York: McGraw-Hill Book Company, 1956), in which he develops the "general adaptation syndrome which causes stress: (1) the alarm stage; (2) the resistant stage; (3) the exhaustion stage."
3. Bill Hybels, *Too Busy Not to Pray* (Downers Grove: InterVarsity Press, 1988), p. 13.

CHAPTER THREE

How to Relax When Only the Tension Is Holding You Together

Of all the things I've lost
It's my mind I miss the most.[1]

"From whence cometh
my help?"
—Psalm 121:1 (KJV)

Do you pray because you need to or because you want to? In the answer to that question we can discover the attitude that made Jesus the master of every potentially stress-producing situation—in other words, daily living.

But before we explore that attitude, it may be helpful to examine a question that was bothering our Bible study group one night. If the intensity of our discussion is any indicator, it's a question that puzzles a lot of people, namely: have you ever wondered why Jesus prayed at all? Why did God the Son have to ask God the Father for help and advice? Behind that question is an even bigger one: who was Jesus Christ? Theologians say He was fully God and fully man, and while a lot of people dutifully nod their assent, they mutter under their breath, "Sure, and He also walked on water, fed thousands of people with practically nothing, made the blind see, and raised the dead. He may have been a man, but He was not an ordinary one like me. He had an edge."

When Jesus emptied Himself, as Paul describes in his famous *kenosis* ("emptying") passage (see Phil. 2:5-11), what actually happened? It's a mystery that theologians have always debated, and probably always will. Whatever it means, we find Jesus praying to His heavenly Father in all kinds of situations, not as much out of need perhaps, but out of desire. Jesus didn't *have* to pray; He *wanted* to pray, and in that simple difference is the secret to the attitude that makes it possible to cope with stress.

When Jesus took the form of a bond servant and was made in the likeness of man, He entered into the limitations of being human, voluntarily, willingly and submissively, intent on only one thing: doing the will of His Father. In that kind of submission was strength and power, and that's why He told the sin-weary crowds:

> Come to me, all you who are weary and
> burdened, and I will give you rest. Take my yoke
> upon you and learn from me, for I am gentle and
> humble in heart, and you will find rest for your
> souls. For my yoke is easy and my burden is light
> (Matt. 11:28-30).

What did Jesus mean by being weary and burdened?
There are several possibilities. He could simply have meant
the burden of sin, which all of us bear from birth. Or, He
could have been referring to the burden of the Law, something very familiar to His Jewish listeners, who knew plenty about having the Pharisees "tie up heavy loads and put
them on men's shoulders" while they themselves were not
"willing to lift a finger to move them" (see Matt. 23:4).

He may have been referring to the grinding heel of
Roman oppression, which kept the Jews gnashing their
teeth most of the time. Or, perhaps He was simply referring to growing weary in a search for a loving, understanding God.

It's possible that Jesus had all four possibilities in mind;
His words give hope for dealing with each of those problems. He was speaking to common people who were
weary and in despair because they knew they were failing
in the search for eternal truth. That's why He offered
them His own kind of yoke. He was saying that you don't
find God by searching for Him. All you really have to do is
pay attention to what God has said and done. In other
words, pay attention to Jesus Christ.[2]

Jesus grasped the attention of his Jewish listeners with
a metaphor they would understand. He invited them to
take His yoke upon their shoulders; in other words, submit to His lordship of their lives. Jesus said His yoke is
easy or, as the Greek word, *chrestos*, means, "well-fitting."

In biblical times, when a farmer needed a yoke for one of his oxen, he would bring the animal into a carpenter's shop and literally have him measured for a new yoke. Then the carpenter would rough out the new piece of equipment and have the farmer bring back the ox to try it

---

Not only does Jesus promise a perfectly fitting yoke, but He offers free lessons on how to use it.

---

on. That way the carpenter could adjust the yoke to be sure it would fit well and not irritate or hamper the ox in any way. In short, yokes were tailor-made to fit oxen.

William Barclay refers to a legend that claims Jesus made the best ox yokes in all of Galilee. He speculates that possibly a sign hung above the door to Jesus' carpenter shop in Nazareth saying, "My yokes fit well."[3]

In this scene, Jesus is at the height of His popularity and He is inviting crowds of followers as well as curiosity seekers to come to Him to wear the kind of yoke that fits human needs and abilities perfectly. Jesus the Son had submitted to the Father and gladly wore His own yoke; now He was inviting all who would listen to submit themselves to Him and be fitted for a yoke that satisfied instead of one that irritated or galled its wearer.

Not only does Jesus promise a perfectly fitting yoke, but He offers free lessons on how to use it. We are to come to Him and learn from His gentle, humble ways. What better means to cope with—and even prevent—the wear and tear of daily stress than this?

And let's not forget that Jesus also said that His burden is light. Common sense tells us He doesn't mean the Christian life is one of simple ease with no challenge or pain involved. All of us face difficult, challenging and sometimes painful burdens from time to time and some people are never rid of them. According to Elton Trueblood, in many cases, "That's where the power lies, living in a tension. You don't play good music on loose strings."4

The trick is to not let the strings become too tight. What Jesus is saying is that any burden can be carried in love, not frustration, anger or despair. Responding to God's love with devotion and gratitude makes the heaviest burden lighter.

Remember Lynn, the mom caught in the parent trap, who secretly wants to drop out of her fast lane and find a permanent parking place? And what about Frank, the freeway fighter, inching along at fifteen miles an hour, while stress eats him alive? How can they ever learn to relax when all that seems to hold them together is the tension of running the rat race? Jesus offers them and us an invitation that has been good for the last twenty centuries. In today's terms, that invitation might sound like this:

> Come unto Me, all ye who battle ungrateful families, impossible schedules, and freeways that are really parking lots, and I will give you rest. Slip into the harness that I have made just for you, so you can pull your load without strain. Submit to Me and learn from Me and you will overcome those packed to-do lists as you cover the long freeway miles. Your schedule may not become any less crowded; clogged freeways you may always have to contend with, but I will be with you, at your side,

helping you pull your load as we seek together to do the Father's will.

Lord, help me to remember that nothing will happen today that You and I can't handle together. Thank You for making my burdens light!

Take a moment to praise God for giving you a yoke that fits perfectly. List some burdens that are easier to carry because you're wearing His yoke and not your own. Or, if you've forgotten to wear Christ's yoke, renew your commitment to do so—right now.

Notes
1. Author unknown. Another bit of bumper sticker wit that dramatizes the stress of the time crunch.
2. William Barclay, *The Daily Study Bible, The Gospel of Matthew,* Vol. 2, (Edinburgh: St. Andrew Press, 1957), p. 17.
3. Ibid., p. 19.
4. Quoted by Elton Trueblood in an interview conducted by Bert Akin, "We Must All Be Ministers," *Eternity,* October 1981, p. 30.

CHAPTER FOUR

Was Jesus a Race Horse or a Turtle?

"The FAX has destroyed any sense of patience or grace that existed. People are so crazy now that they call to tell you your FAX line is busy."

—Josh Baron, Hollywood Publicist[1]

"For a thousand years in thy sight are...as a watch in the night."

—Psalm 90:4 (*KJV*)

While chatting informally one day with a group of medical colleagues, Dr. Hans Selye good-naturedly agreed to sum up thirty years of work on stress research by giving them his three-step "secret recipe" for dealing with life.

The first ingredient is: *Decide if you are a "race horse" or a "turtle."* Take honest inventory to recognize your own limits. Race horses are the Type *A* people who charge through life exhilarated by working fast, hard and long. Without the fast lane and chock-full to-do lists, the day is a wasted bore.

At the other end of the spectrum are the turtles—Type *B* folks who do not tap their fingers on the steering wheel at stoplights, take their time and don't need to complete a long list of to-do's to make their day worthwhile. Type *B*s nod knowingly when they hear reports saying heart disease drops 30 percent in people who take a thirty-minute nap every day.[2]

Like most people, you probably feel you fall somewhere between these two extremes. Nonetheless, everyone leans in one direction or the other and you should take that into account as you set your daily goals and priorities, which is the second ingredient in Dr. Selye's recipe: *Choose your own goals in life.* Be sure you know they're your goals, not something forced on you by your family, friends or peer group.

Goal setting has become a separate institution in recent years. You can attend all kinds of goal-setting classes, seminars or workshops and read many different books on setting long-range goals, intermediate goals and short-range goals. We will look at goals more closely in later chapters, but to restate Dr. Selye's first two ingredients in his secret recipe for handling stress as principles for living:

1. Know who you are and how you operate best.

2. Know what you want to do and become and set your goals accordingly.

The ultimate model for both of these principles is Jesus Christ. Neither a race horse nor a turtle, Jesus set His own goals and moved steadily toward them at His own pace. When He dropped by to see Mary and Martha that day (see Luke 10:38-42), it was obvious who was who: Martha was Type *A*, Mary was Type *B*; Martha was the race horse, Mary was the turtle.

When Jesus commended Mary for sitting quietly at His feet and choosing the better part, was He disapproving the race horses who tend to take charge, take action and get things done? Not exactly. If there was ever a take-charge-and-get-things-done kind of person, it was Jesus. But He did it with a pace that was never hurried, harried or hassled. He just did it, quietly and effectively, always depending on His heavenly Father in every circumstance (see John 5:17-21; 6:44; 8:28,29).

A few months after Jesus' visit to their home, Mary and Martha saw a striking example of how He did things at His own pace. Jesus and the twelve were "across the Jordan," near the place where John had baptized so many nearly three years before, including Jesus on that day when the Spirit descended on Him like a dove and the Father's voice was heard to say He was well-pleased with the Son (see Mark 1:9-11).

But John was dead now, beheaded by Herod for his fearless condemnation of Herod's adulterous sins. And time seemed to be running out for Jesus, as well. He was on the "most wanted" list back in Jerusalem where the religious authorities plotted His death. Jesus had slipped across the Jordan to gather strength for His final ordeal, but as usual people followed Him and He continued to do miraculous works of healing, even while He tried to rest.

It was during these days of peace before the storm that a messenger brought word from Mary and Martha that their brother, Lazarus, was deathly ill. Today, when a doctor or surgeon gets a "Code Blue," he dashes to the victim's side to give what help he can, but Jesus merely said that Lazarus' illness would not end in death and that God would be glorified. Jesus could have healed Lazarus "long distance" just as He did the centurion's servant (see Luke 7:1-10), but He chose to take a different route. Seemingly unconcerned, He stayed right where He was for two more days before telling His disciples, "Let us go back to Judea" (see John 11:1-7).

The disciples were aghast. To go back to Judea meant certain death for Jesus, perhaps the rest of them, as well. When the disciples reminded Jesus that the last time He had been in Judea, the Jews had tried to stone Him, the Lord answered with a parabolic observation about time and how to use it to best advantage:

> Are there not twelve hours of daylight? A man who walks by day will not stumble, for he sees by this world's light. It is when he walks by night that he stumbles, for he has no light (John 11:9,10).

John's Gospel contains many statements with two meanings and this is one of them. On the surface, Jesus is reminding His disciples of how time was allotted in those days, by the Jews as well as the Romans: twelve hours for the day and twelve for night. Twelve hours was supposed to provide time enough to accomplish what was necessary for any given day.[3]

Jesus seems to be stating a simple truth: while the sun is shining you can see what you are doing and where you

are going. When the sun goes down, it's time for all jour-
neying and work to cease. But there is still more to be
learned in His reference to "the light." Jesus often referred
to Himself as *the light of the world.* At a deeper level, He is
reminding His disciples *there is only so much time to appre-*

We don't have any time to waste on trying to be someone we are not and trying to reach goals that aren't what God has in mind for us.

---

ciate and accept Him, the True Light for all men and
women.

Then Jesus went on to say his friend Lazarus was
"asleep" and that He had to go back to wake him up. In
their typical literal fashion, the disciples thought Jesus
meant natural sleep, but then He told them plainly that
Lazarus was dead and that He was glad He hadn't been
there because now they would see something that would
increase their faith.

Speaking for the whole group, Thomas said with resignation, but also with real courage: "Let us also go that we
may die with Him."

The rest of the story is better known: Jesus arrives to
find Lazarus has been dead for four days. The stage is set
to glorify God with a special miracle at a special time,
with the Cross an imminent possibility. Now He will help
His disciples understand what He was saying about the
light of the world who is in their midst.

Jesus asks that the stone be rolled away and then He

puts death at bay with a shout: "Lazarus, come out!" And Lazarus—whose name means "God is my help"—walks out of his grave. The deed is done; Jesus has reached His goal—to glorify God—and He has done it according to His own schedule, moving neither too fast nor too slowly.

Again, Jesus models principles for helping us cope with the time famine of the latter days of the twentieth century. With almost every labor- and time-saving convenience imaginable, and with more leisure than any society in history, we still don't have enough time to live it all. As one national magazine put it, "Sure enough, the computers are byting, the satellites spinning, the Cuisinarts whizzing, just as planned. Yet we are ever out of breath."[4]

Although He was not "blessed" with telephones, freeways and fax machines, Jesus faced a "time famine" of His own. He could have dashed breathlessly about Palestine trying to "get it all done," but He didn't. Instead, He knew exactly who He was and what He was trying to do, and He did it according to an agenda that He set carefully and prayerfully with His heavenly Father.

Oh, that we might do the same! Yes, there are pressures and schedules and demands from every direction, but as Jesus told His disciples, there are but twelve hours in a day and the same is true for us. We live in the age of the time clock, when many work the "swing shift" or "graveyard." We carve up our days a bit differently than they did in the first century, but Jesus' principle is firm. *We have plenty of time to do the work God has given us to do*; but when that allotted time is gone, it is gone. We don't have any time to waste on trying to be someone we are not and trying to reach goals that aren't what God has in mind for us.

Avoiding both these pitfalls is good strategy for handling stress, but there is one more ingredient in Dr. Hans Selye's recipe. His "secret seasoning," which makes life taste truly delicious and even more stress free, is in the next chapter.

————————

Lord, show me my limits as well as my abilities.
Help me set my goals to glorify You, no one else.

————————

What do you see in your life that tells you if you are mostly race horse or mostly turtle? Do your goals match your personality and abilities? Do you need to slow down or speed up?

Notes
1. Nancy Gibbs, "How America Has Run Out of Time," *Time*, April 24, 1989, p. 60.
2. Reported by the University of Athens Medical School, Greece, quoted in *Bottom Line*, November 15, 1989, p. 1.
3. William Barclay, *The Gospel of John, The Daily Study Bible*, Vol. 2 (Edinburgh: St. Andrew Press, 1955), p. 97.
4. Nancy Gibbs, p. 59.

CHAPTER FIVE

The Golden Rule for Stress Control

"Life moves pretty fast, and if you don't stop and look around once in a while, you are going to miss it."

—Ferris Bueller[1]

"The steps of a good man are ordered by the Lord."

—Psalm 37:23 (KJV)

When Dr. Hans Selye shared his "secret recipe" for handling the stresses of life with some colleagues one day (see chapter four), his first two ingredients were typical of basic "stress advice":

1. Know your limits;
2. Set proper goals that fit you, not somebody else.

You can find all kinds of similar ideas for controlling stress in good books or articles covering the subject. For example:

- Exercise regularly. The better shape you're in, the better your body handles stress. Exercise actually increases endorphins, which are a natural tranquilizer.
- Get enough sleep. Mothers of young children may laugh hysterically at such naive advice. Nonetheless, moms should do all they can to catch up on sleep when possible, instead of trying to do a lot of extra chores when they finally do get the kids down.
- Be flexible. The more flexible you are the less frustrated you will become.
- Do not hurry. It only speeds up the wear and tear on your body and mind. If you do better planning and organizing of your time, you will do less hurrying—and be less stressed.
- Don't lose your temper (nobody else wants it anyway). There are constructive ways to deal with anger; one of the best is through forgiveness.
- Don't sweat the small stuff. The little hassles of life can kill you faster than the big ones.

The above are just a few of dozens of techniques you can find for fighting stress.[2] The third ingredient in Dr. Selye's recipe—which he called his "secret seasoning"—is different. Instead of a technique, it is really a strategy that Selye described as "altruistic egotism—looking out for

---

It's not a question of trying to avoid stress, but trying to balance your life so that the good stress far outweighs the bad.

---

oneself by being necessary to others and earning their good will."

Selye cautioned that we must balance altruism and egotism carefully because either one can be pushed to an extreme. If you overdo altruism, you can literally work yourself to death trying to please others. If you overemphasize egotism, the obvious result is the "looking out for Number One" mentality.

Selye suggested a middle ground and admitted that his concept sounded an awful lot like the Golden Rule taught by Jesus Christ:

> So in everything, do to others what you would have them do to you, for this sums up the Law and the Prophets (Matt. 7:12).

Possibly the best known of all Jesus' teachings, the Golden Rule, strikes a perfect balance between indulging your ego (conceit and selfishness) and starving it (false humility and self-depreciation).

Many religions claim to teach the Golden Rule, but only Jesus put it in its positive form. Other religions and philosophies put it negatively. For example, the rabbis of Jesus' day taught: "What is hateful to yourself, do to no other." Confucius said: "What you do not want done to yourself, do not do to others."[3]

In its negative form, the Golden Rule is the kind of common sense that makes a law-abiding society possible. The law says, "Don't hurt others because you don't want to be hurt yourself." The Golden Rule says: "Go out of your way to help others because you, too, like and want and need to be helped."

The Golden Rule is the foundation of the royal law of Scripture: "Love your neighbor as yourself" (see Jas. 2:8). At the very least, we can get through life being careful not to do what may hurt others; but it's another matter to do good and right things out of love, with no hidden agenda.

Common sense sometimes (often) tells us not to go out of our way for others. At worst, going out of your way can make life complicated, difficult and even dangerous. At best, you will have less time to spend on your own activities and responsibilities.

How then does the Golden Rule help us avoid stress? Remember, all of life is stress. It's not a question of trying to avoid stress, but trying to balance your life so that the good stress far outweighs the bad. Going out of your way to help others is a source of good stress because afterward you almost always feel gratified, inspired and strengthened.

When Hans Selye gave his recipe for handling stress to his colleagues, he wasn't trying to teach biblical truth. He was simply sharing some practical ideas that he had gathered in over thirty years on researching stress and what it does to the human mind and body. But as is almost always true, practical ideas have their roots in the principles from Scripture. Practice the Golden Rule and you will have less distress and more good stress. For example:

- Instead of thinking only of furthering your own ambitions, you relax and let God worry about your next promotion, or who gets named chairperson of that important committee.
- Instead of cutting corners to make a deadline, a quota or a deal, you stick to the high road, and wind up with less pressure and stress.
- Instead of exacting revenge, you forgive and try to forget because you know a grudge is a stressful burden to carry.

A few years ago, Lee Buck, a former top insurance sales executive, wrote a book to demonstrate the Golden Rule in action in the toughest of all arenas: the business world. In a chapter he calls "The Principle of Turning the Other Shoulder Blade," he tells of how a colleague stabbed him in the back, spreading untrue rumors throughout the company. Buck said nothing, and four years later he became a regional president in charge of all divisional managers including, yes—you guessed it—the colleague who had done him dirt.

Now Buck faced a decision. He could practice the business world's "code of revenge" and make this man's life miserable, or he could practice the Golden Rule. Buck chose the Golden Rule and he did everything he could to help the man, from getting clearance on new policy formulations to standing behind him in any decision he made. After all, although the man had had his problems, he was still a good insurance salesman, and Buck determined that he would help him become an even better one.

At first the man was suspicious, but later he realized

Buck was sincere and wound up inviting Buck and his wife to his new home for a weekend visit, which turned out to be a very pleasant time. As the years went by, Buck's former enemy became his friend and one of the best divisional managers in the company, who went about saying, "If you ever need help from someone in the home office, the guy to count on is Lee Buck."[4]

Buck admits that earlier in his career it might have been natural to try to get revenge on the colleague who had done him dirt, but that would only have hurt both of them. Buck cites an elemental law as sure as gravity: "If you put someone down, you sink right along with him." The Golden rule would say, "If you raise someone up, you rise right along with him."[5]

It is a much less stressful way to live.

Lord, the world says those who have the gold make the rules. Keep reminding me that the Golden Rule has nothing to do with grasping and gathering, but everything to do with giving and letting go.

With whom do you need to practice the Golden Rule right now? How will this lessen stress in your life?

Notes
1. From the film, *Ferris Bueller's Day Off.*
2. Adapted from Archibald E. Hart, "Suggestions: Preventing Burnout and Stress," *Theology News and Notes*, March, 1984, p. 20.
3. William Barclay, *The Daily Study Bible, The Gospel of Matthew*, Vol. 1 (Edinburgh: The St. Andrew Press, 1956), pp. 277-278.
4. See Lee Buck with Dick Schneider, *Tapping Your Secret Source of Power* (Old Tappan: Fleming H. Revell Company, 1985), pp. 33-37.
5. Ibid, p. 37.

CHAPTER SIX

Who Keeps Shaking the Balance Beam of Life?

Lord, just think of me as a
tightrope walker
who had a bad bit of luck.
—*Prayers for Pagans and Hypocrites*[1]

"For the Lord knoweth the way
of the righteous: but the way of
the ungodly shall perish."
—Psalm 1:6 *(KJV)*

Balance.

In a time-poor culture like our own, there are few who don't seek balance, fewer still who feel they attain it for very long at a time.

The dictionary will tell you that balance is a state of equilibrium, which can be physical, mental or emotional. To "strike a balance" is to reach or achieve a state or position between two extremes.[2]

For a vivid example of physical balance, all we need to picture is a tightrope walker or one of those gymnasts who perform on the balance beam during the Olympics. What they do in a world only four inches wide is a mind-boggling definition of balance in action.

The mental and emotional side of balance is harder to grasp. As we try to juggle our minutes and fit them into hours that don't seem long enough, at least four major areas come into play:

- Our vocation (or avocation);
- Our relationships, particularly the family;
- Our social and recreational activities;
- Our spiritual dimension, which begins and ends with God.

Linda sighs as she grabs the jangling phone for the fifteenth time that morning. It isn't easy trying to run a business from home. People simply don't take it seriously and they think nothing of calling several times a day "just to chat." With all these interruptions, how can she ever meet her deadlines?

"Linda, it's Jane. Are you busy?"

Linda bites her tongue and swallows a sarcastic answer. What does Jane think she is doing, watching "Days of Our Lives" while spooning down a pint of Häagen-Dazs? Jane knows she works every spare second. A few more projects like this one and they can pay off the MasterCard bill and start saving for a new mini-van to replace the old station wagon, which lately has made driving almost as suspenseful as Russian roulette.

"Actually, yes," Linda answers. "I've got a project due tomorrow."

"Oh, I'm sorry, but I'm really in a bind and I don't know what I'll do."

Linda smiles. Jane could be a travel agent for guilt trips. She knows I won't leave her hanging...might as well find out what she wants. "Well, I'm never too busy to help a friend; what can I do for you, Jane?"

"Oh, if you could possibly work it out, I'd be so grateful. I know it's my turn to pick up the kids at school today, but I just remembered I'm supposed to be at a special meeting of the worship committee at church. Miss Baldwin is the chairman and she has to go out of town, and we must get some things settled, and this is the only time available. If I don't show up, I'll be on her black list."

What can I do? Linda wonders. If I say no, it sounds as if I'm against worship and prayer. But it's just not fair. Jane doesn't have to work and she attends every Bible study, prayer meeting and committee she can find.

Glancing quickly at the stack of work on her desk, Jane mentally notes that she can probably stay up late and finish it after everyone else is in bed. Then she says, "Sure, Jane, I can rearrange things. I'll pick up the kids today and you get to that meeting."

"Oh, thanks, Linda. I really appreciate this. Hope you get your work done on time!"

Linda is about to hang up when she hears Jane's voice continue. "By the way, Linda, I know your career is important to you, but it would really do you so much good to get away now and then. Why don't you think about going with me to women's Bible study next week? Pray about it and I'll call you later!"

Shrugging her shoulders and rolling her eyes, Linda goes back to her desk. There is still a little more than an hour before school is out. Maybe she can salvage some of the day and get something accomplished.

Sometimes Jane can talk like an inconsiderate air head, *but she means well,* Linda muses to herself. *Maybe I am too busy, but I love my work and it's a release, not a boring grind. Is it so wrong to want to work,* especially when *I'm balancing my job with my home and family? I spend more time with my kids than Jane does with hers. Let Jane attend her Bible studies if* she has to. *Right now I just don't have the extra hours to spare.*

So Linda, a prototype heroine based on different wives I've interviewed while researching this book, plunges on into the rest of her day, convinced she is doing fine up there on her personal balance beam. But is she? If Jesus of Nazareth dropped by to interrupt her busy day, what might He say? It's quite likely He would use His favorite method of passing on a word to the wise—the parable. And in Linda's case, He might have chosen the story of the rich fool, which could also be entitled "The Ballad of an Unbalanced Man":

> The ground of a certain rich man produced a good crop. He thought to himself, "What shall I do? I have no place to store my crops."
>
> Then he said, "This is what I'll do. I will tear down my barns and build bigger ones, and there I will store all my grain and my goods." And I'll say to myself, "You have plenty of good things laid up for many years. Take life easy; eat, drink and be merry."

But God said to him, "You fool! This very night your life will be demanded from you. Then who will get what you have prepared for yourself?"

This is how it will be with anyone who stores up things for himself but is not rich toward God (Luke 12:16-21).

With very little trouble we can make several observations about the rich fool and his unbalanced life.

Whenever we shove God to the background and live for ourselves, we are victims of an unbalanced life.

He was self-centered and short-sighted, all wrapped up in himself, never seeing beyond his own little world. He was a hedonist who tried to play God, but the Lord had the last word. Calling the man a fool, God told him his life would end that very night and he would leave his earthly riches behind. In the final sentence of the parable, we find the key words that point toward the balanced life: "This is how it will be with anyone who stores up things for himself but is not rich toward God."

Jesus is not saying earthly riches are bad per se; neither does He say that pleasure and relaxation are not allowed. And despite His refusal to arbitrate the inheritance problems of a man in the crowd (see Luke 12:13-15), He is not saying that it is wrong to be involved with inheritances and business matters of all kinds.

What Jesus is saying is that whenever we shove God to

the background and live for ourselves, we are victims of an unbalanced life.

What about Linda and Jane? Neither one of them is exactly in the rich man's shoes, but they both should be concerned about following in his footsteps. If Linda has no time for Bible study or prayer because she's too busy "balancing" her career with taking care of her family, is she rich or poor? If Jane fails to spend enough time with her children because she's attending too many church meetings and other get-togethers, is she growing rich toward God or growing rich in religious activities?

Only Linda and Jane can answer those questions for themselves, and the same is true of you and me. Balance is a very personal thing, but it helps to have a Partner. Then the balance beam will always be rock solid.

Lord, help me remember You are not one more thing I must balance with everything else; as Paul said, in You I live, move, have my being—and keep my balance.

Review the four basic areas of life. Where are you in balance? Where are you shaky?

Vocation/avocation:_____

_____

_____

_____

Relationships (friends/family): Social/recreational: _____

_____

_____

_____

Spiritual: _____

_____

_____

_____

Notes

1. Peter DeRosa, *Prayers for Pagans and Hypocrites* (New York: William Morrow and Company, Inc., 1977), p. 95.
2. William Morris, editor, *The American Heritage Dictionary of the English Language* (Boston: American Heritage Publishing Company, Inc., and Houghton Mifflin Company, 1969), pp. 100-101.

CHAPTER SEVEN

He Who Has Ears, Hears What He Chooses

There may be a heaven;
There must be a hell;
Meanwhile, we have our
life here—
Well?

—Anonymous[1]

"Cause me to hear thy
lovingkindness...for in thee
do I trust."

—Psalm 143:8 *(KJV)*

An Indian was in downtown New York, walking along with his friend, who lived in New York City. Suddenly he said, "I hear a cricket."

"Oh, you're crazy," his friend replied.

"No, I hear a cricket. I do! I'm sure of it."

"It's the noon hour. You know there are people bustling around, cars honking, taxis squealing, noises from the city. I'm sure you can't hear a cricket."

"I'm sure I do." He listened attentively and then walked to the corner, across the street, and looked all around. Finally on the other corner he found a shrub in a large cement planter. He dug beneath the leaf and found a cricket.

His friend was duly astounded. But the Indian said, "No. My ears are no different from yours. It simply depends on what you are listening to. Here, let me show you."

He reached into his pocket and pulled out a handful of change—a few quarters, some dimes, nickels and pennies. Then he dropped it all on the concrete.

Every head within a block turned.

"You see what I mean?" the Indian said as he began picking up his coins. "It all depends on what you are listening for."[2]

What we are listening for reveals a lot about how we are handling our time and our lives. Television, radios, traffic, crowds, people everywhere—it all drowns out God's still, small voice—unless, of course, we can be like the Indian and tune in to hear it, even in the busy din of daily living.

The other morning, while scribbling some thoughts for this chapter, I came up with: "A balanced life demands careful juggling of labor and leisure, relationships and reflection." Before adding the period to this sentence, I realized my choice of the word "juggling" had betrayed my own problem. But I suspect I am not alone. A lot of people are juggling the pieces and parts of their lives, hoping they can keep all the balls in the air without fumbling their responsibilities.

Thorny ground believers have no time for spiritual reflection, because their lives are too crowded with other things.

The word "juggling" pictures someone who is very busy, intent on not missing a thing. We do pretty well at juggling our labor, but leisure can easily get dropped along the way. I talked to a friend the other day after church, and mentioned I hadn't seen him for a while. He told me he and his wife had been on a cruise to the Caribbean, but he was quick to let me know that it was the first vacation that they'd had in several years. Perhaps he thought a cruise vacation sounded extravagant and he wanted to justify it—I'm not sure—but I was more concerned by the fact he had run the rat race for so long without more than an occasional weekend off here and there.

At the other extreme, some people live for the weekend, with or without the Michelob. They dislike their work and seem to develop energy for going back on Monday only because of the fun or diversion they find away from their jobs on Saturday and Sunday.

Add relationships to your daily juggling act and things get even more complicated. It takes time to build and maintain relationships, but the clock is a ruthless taskmaster. One of the biggest casualties of the time famine is the American family. Trying to do justice to their jobs and to their children is more than many parents can handle. One psychologist believes, "We're at the breaking point as far as family is concerned."[3]

As the day begins, a typical American family resembles a covey of quail ready to blast forth from its nest in all directions—to catch school buses, car pools, or maybe a cab to the airport. Hallmark, ever aware of the pressures on those "Who care enough to send the very best," now puts out cards you can slip into your child's lunch box, urging him or her to: "HAVE A SUPER DAY AT SCHOOL!"

By the time we get to the ball called reflection, we have hardly the time or energy to pick it up, because too many other things have occupied our hectic day. As one Baptist retreat coordinator put it, "We suffer today the pollution of activity, especially the pollution of unreflective living. We do and do, go and go, talk and talk...and just for a moment, we wonder, 'What does it all mean?'"[4]

For one thing it means we are failing to stop and listen. On at least six different occasions, Jesus said, "He who hath ears to hear, let him hear."[5] Consider, for example, this well-known parable:

> A farmer went out to sow his seed. As he was scattering the seed, some fell along the path, and the birds came and ate it up. Some fell on rocky places, where it did not have much soil. It sprang up quickly, because the soil was shallow. But when the sun came up, the plants were scorched, and they withered because they had no root. Other seed fell among thorns, which grew up and choked the plants. Still other seed fell on good soil, where it

produced a crop—a hundred, sixty or thirty times what was sown (Matt. 13:3-8).

This parable is called by different names. Some refer to it as the Parable of the Sower, others as the Parable of the Soils. If you seek a balanced life, the "Parable of the Soils" is best because it reminds you that God wants fruit in your life.

Anyone seeking the balanced life should focus especially on what it means to be thorny ground because it's here many believers find themselves choking on their busy schedules, which, ironically enough, are supposed to attest to their high productivity. Thorny-ground believers have no time for spiritual reflection, because their lives are too crowded with other things.

It is easy to get so busy there is never a spare moment to think about how balanced or unbalanced we really are. The devotional life, in particular, is the first thing that is often skipped or squeezed into "seven minutes a day." We pray on the run, giving God His to-do list and asking Him to please hurry so we can stay on schedule.

Sometimes, however, God's still, small voice brings us up short in dramatic ways. Dean Merrill, vice president of Publications for Focus on the Family, was shocked when a doctor told him he had a duodenal ulcer, and that he had better examine his life-style and work schedule. Fortunately for Merrill, it was a turning point in his life.

"I decided," he writes, "that although I wouldn't become lazy, I would from then on refuse to be stampeded. In the face of pressure, I would take deeper breaths and take control of my pace."[6]

That was over fifteen years ago. The ulcer went away and hasn't been back since because Dean Merrill had ears to hear God's still small voice in the doctor's warning.

If the pace of life seems to have you off balance, consider the Parable of the Soils, especially the part about thorns choking out a believer's growth and maturity. The parable mentions "the cares, the riches and the pleasures of this life," but as Lloyd Ogilvie points out, these words "are but headings for long lists of priorities we bring to the Christian life or keep long after we have accepted Christ as Lord."[7]

You probably don't have an ulcer, but you do face plenty of stress, so keep Dean Merrill's solution in mind: Refuse to be stampeded by the particular pressures that pack your days. Ask God to control your pace and you will bear the fruit He desires: thirty- sixty- and even a hundredfold.

Those who have ears to hear, let them hear.

Lord, I confess that I've let some weeds and thorns grow unnoticed in my life. Uproot them now and help me refuse to be stampeded into running the rat race without taking time for spiritual reflection.

Evaluate how you are handling your labor, your leisure, your relationships and your reflection. Where are you spending too much time and where are you spending too little? How is overemphasis on one or more areas of your life causing thorns and weeds to choke your fruitfulness? Do you know any "hundredfold" Christians? Where do you think you fall on the scale? List at least one step you can take to clear away the thorns and become more fruitful.

Notes

1. Quoted by Frank S. Mead, editor and compiler, *The Encyclopedia of Religious Quotations* (Old Tappan: Fleming H. Revell Company, 1965), p. 267.
2. Source unknown, quoted by Tim Hansel, *When I Relax I Feel Guilty* (Elgin, IL: David C. Cook Publishing Company, 1979), p. 146.
3. Yale University Professor Edward Zigler, quoted by Nancy Gibbs, "How America Has Run Out of Time," Time, April 24, 1989, p. 58.
4. Bill Clemmons, quoted by Dean Merrill, "Stampeding to Tomorrow," "Editors, Etc.," *Christian Herald*, April 1989, p. 2.
5. See Matt. 13:9,43; Mark 4:23, 7:16; Luke 14:35.
6. Dean Merrill, "Stampeding to Tomorrow," *Christian Herald*, April 1989, p. 2.
7. Lloyd Ogilvie, *Autobiography of God* (Ventura: Regal Books, 1979), p. 61.

CHAPTER EIGHT

Do Nice Guys Even Finish?

I have ambition, by which sin,
the angels fell;
I climbed and, step by step,
O Lord,
Ascended into hell.
—W. H. Davies[1]

"I would rather be a doorkeeper
in the house of my God than
dwell in the tents of the
wicked."
—Psalm 84:10

"Nice guys finish last!"

You may have heard this well-known maxim, uttered by baseball legend Leo Durocher. Leo's candor caught the imagination of much of the American public and his "nice guys finish last" quip became a cynical byword for a lot of people who perceived the rat race as a rat-eat-rat proposition.

Then, in the 1970s, an irreverent real estate salesman named Robert Ringer burst onto the best-seller scene with titles that shocked but then titillated the public's imagination. In books like *Winning Through Intimidation* and *Looking Out for Number One*, Ringer strongly hinted that nice guys might not even finish at all. His "three-type theory" held that there are only three kinds of people in the business world:

The Type 1s are the people who play no games. From the beginning they let you know they want to win and plan to "take all your chips." You always know where they stand.

Type 2 people have a hidden agenda. They assure you that winning isn't important; in fact, they insist they are trying to help you get everything "that's coming to you." Then, of course, Type 2s go for the jugular and try to beat you any way they can.

Type 3s are the most dangerous species of all. Like Type 2s, they assure you that winning is not important and actually think they mean it. Later, however, Type 3s try to do you in with any number of very personal interpretations of what's right and what's wrong.

The bottom line: Type 3s try to take all your chips, too, but they rationalize everything while doing so.[2]

Let's face it: Ringer's cynical view of the "three types of people in the world" is far more accurate than we want to admit. In fact, we may have dealt with a few Christians who fall into the Type 3 category (maybe Types 2 and 1, for that matter). And, if we want to be honest, perhaps you and I have played footsie with these behaviors ourselves, especially Type 3. The eye of the beholder prefers to see what it wants to see, and, to paraphrase something Jesus said, "If your vision is a bit fuzzy, it can foul up a lot of things" (see Matt. 6:23).

How do we balance living and competing in this world with the desire to do God's will? Is it wrong to be ambitious in any sense of the word? When does ambition turn into self-destruction? If there is such a thing as "Christian ambition," what does it look, feel and sound like?

- Michael wants that promotion so badly he can taste it. Not only does it mean more money and perks, but it also means security. The only problem is, Frank is up for that promotion, too. He hasn't been with the company nearly as long as Michael, but he's sharp and everything he touches turns to black ink on the bottom line. Just a few days ago, however, Frank's past came to light. Michael learned about Frank's police record when a friend who works for the D.A.'s office inadvertently talked out of turn.

  Now Michael struggles with what to do. As a faithful church member, he has always believed in "doing unto others as you'd have them do unto you." But every time he tries to pray for guidance on this one, the ceiling closes in. Doesn't Frank's boss have a right to know about Frank's record? Doesn't Michael have a right to the division manager job, since he's been with the company so much longer? Wouldn't he be doing everyone a favor to tell the truth?

• Andy fingers the manila envelope in his hand, trying to decide if he should open it. His friend John, an honor student, has just handed him that envelope, saying with a wink and a smile, "I know you've been having a little trouble with calculus. Here's a copy of the next test; you can use it to even things up."

When Andy tried to protest, John just scoffed, saying, "Look, I know you want to get on the honor roll because your dad wants you to go to State next year. What's the matter with getting a little preview? Sometimes you have to stretch it a little to get by in life, so why not go for it? Everybody else does."

Yes, why not go for it? Andy knows that a lot of kids in his Christian high school cheat, or at least cut corners to get better grades. As John told him once, "Why settle for a C or even a B, when you can get an A and a higher paying job some day? Isn't that what it's all about?"

• "Honey, I know Mommy promised to take you and your sister to the zoo on Saturday, but something's come up at work and I just can't get away. I've got to go now. Try not to call me any more this afternoon; I'll be home later and we can talk about it."

Joyce hangs up the phone with a sigh. Being a single parent of two daughters isn't easy, and when you mix it with being the first woman vice-president of First National Bank, it's even tougher. *Why do I feel so guilty?* Joyce wonders as she turns back to her desk full of loan applications. I get the very best child care for the girls and I am usually home every evening. But this meeting on Saturday is important, and I need to be there to hold up my end. I'll just have to hope the girls understand....

All of the people in the scenes above have one thing in common—ambition, that eager or strong desire to

---

Jesus taught His followers to become people who find greatness and success in serving others instead of personal gain.

---

achieve and succeed. It's interesting to check the origins of ambition and find that it comes from the Latin *ambire*, which means "to go around." To be ambitious is a quality the world approves of, but it is also an invitation to becoming a Type 3 person, who knows what's right, but is willing to "go around" whatever is in the way in order to succeed.

Ambition reared its seductive head in the midst of Jesus' disciples more than once. On one occasion, James and John, the sons of Zebedee, come to Jesus with a special request, asking Him to let them sit at His right and at His left in His glory. When James and John talk about Jesus' "glory," they aren't asking for heavenly rewards. They're still under the impression that Christ's kingdom will be an earthly one and they want a major piece of the action. But Jesus never planned any earthly kingdoms, only a heavenly one, and He tells James and John that all the seats of honor are to be assigned by His heavenly Father and no one else.

In this scene, James and John come off looking like ambitious bad guys, but the other ten disciples are no less aspiring. When the others hear about the request by the brothers, they're indignant. In fact, it gets so tense, Jesus feels it necessary to call them all together for a little lesson on "inverted values," and He says:

> You know that those who are regarded as rulers of the Gentiles lord it over them, and their high officials exercise authority over them. Not so with you. Instead, whoever wants to become great among you must be your servant, and whoever wants to be first must be slave of all. For even the Son of Man did not come to be served, but to serve, and to give His life as a ransom for many (Mark 10:42-45).

In a few words, Christ tells His disciples how to temper ambition with commitment, as He turns the meaning of greatness upside down. In the world, the question is, "How many people do you manage, oversee or control?" In Jesus' kingdom, the question is, "How many people do you serve, wait upon and help, sacrificing your own interests and ambitions?"

Life is full of all of Robert Ringer's types of people. Type 1 comes right at you and tries to beat you. Type 2 claims he wants you to win, but don't turn your back. Type 3 tries to tell you (and himself) that he's a good fellow and he's only trying to do "what's right," as he puts his own ambitions ahead of everything and everyone else.

Jesus, however, taught His followers to become Type

4s—people who find greatness and success in serving others instead of personal gain. This isn't an easy way to go. Usually, it is difficult, inconvenient and it could even cost a vice-presidency along the way. But Type 4 people never lose their balance. Their model is Jesus Himself, who "did not come to be served, but to serve." (Matt. 20:28). They know that nice guys always finish, and they always finish best.

———

Lord, You know I have ambition. Help me turn that ambition into servanthood and leave where I finish up to You.

———

Take out a sheet of paper and list your "ambitions" (or, if you prefer, call them "goals"). Does fulfilling any of these ambitions mean that you may have to cut a corner in some way? Or, can you use Jesus' strategy for fulfilling your ambitions through being a servant?

Notes
1. W. H. Davies, Ambition, quoted in *The Pocketbook of Quotations*, edited by Henry Davidoff (New York: Pocketbooks, 1942), p. 4.
2. See Robert Ringer, *Winning Through Intimidation* (New York: Fawcett Crest Books, 1974), pp. 60-62.

CHAPTER NINE

But What if the Other Rats Are Faster

"Winning isn't everything,
but losing is nothing."
—Tommy LaSorda

"If the Lord had not been on
our side...they would have
swallowed us alive."
—Psalm 124:2,3

Steve sat in a group of his baby boomer peers pondering the inner tensions of anyone born into that "blip" of seventy-six million that swelled the American population between the late '40s and early '60s. His conflict was that of any typical Christian trying to balance spiritual convictions with the demands of "life in the real world."

There are always those competitors who are only too happy to give free reign to their "killer instincts."

"How do I reconcile my goals to achieve something from Monday through Friday with the desire to do God's will?" Steve wanted to know. "I'm competing with nine or ten other people at work for the same job and some of them are really sharp. If I want to advance, I've got to be quicker and better than they are, but at the same time I don't want to feel as if I'm being cutthroat or greedy."

Steve is caught on the horns of a familiar dilemma. He wants to win, but not at anyone else's expense. Steve wonders, "Is there a way to compete in this win/lose society and act as a Christian should?"

Perhaps there is. Denis Waitley believes that competition isn't the problem, it's how we compete that counts. He writes:

> Competition—be it in the marketplace, polling place, or playing place—sharpens skills, exposes poor and shoddy efforts, stands guard against goug-

ing and greed, and motivates us to be the best we can be. But what is missing in today's win/lose society is the spirit of cooperation and creativity, a feeling that it is more important to help everyone develop his or her potential as a human being rather than simply get on the score board and add another win to the victory column.[1]

Donald Seibert, who for years served as Chief Operating Officer of the J. C. Penney Company, never stuck his head in the sand. Seibert was well aware that there are always those competitors who are only too happy to give free reign to their "killer instincts." But Seibert never gave in to that kind of "tooth and claw" thinking. In *The Ethical Executive,* a book he co-authored with William Proctor, Seibert wrote:

> The successful people I know aren't obsessed with beating out the other person and stepping on others' heads to get to the top. Their motivation, instead, is to do such a good job at their assigned tasks that they come to be regarded as first in a fast field of excellent talent. In fact, the better your competitors do, the better it makes you look if you win first place.[2]

But what if you don't finish first? The "winning isn't everything, it's the only thing" philosophy that has pervaded American sports seldom remembers who finished second. The Olympic games, once the proud bastion of "be all you can be," have turned into a free-for-all to "get all the gold you can." The original Olympic spirit had a two-fold goal: you were to develop your own ability, yes, but you also never forgot that you had a collective responsibility to help others develop theirs as well.

One of the finest demonstrations of this "double win" philosophy occurred in the 1984 winter games at Sarajevo, Yugoslavia. The men's slalom competition was coming to a close and the Mahre twins, Steve and Phil, were in their final competition for the U.S. Phil made his two slalom runs first and wound up with a time of 1:39:41, which put him in first place. Then it was Steve's turn.

Born only minutes apart, the twins had always been intense competitors, so what should Phil do at a time like this? The win/lose approach would suggest that he stand quietly by and watch his brother make his run down an icy slope that was getting more difficult every second. Instead, Phil grabbed a Walkie-Talkie and radioed advice to Steve, telling him how to make the fastest and safest run he could.

Steve took Phil's advice but still had difficulty with some of the turns. He wound up .21 second behind, good enough for the silver. Reporters crowded in and asked him what his brother had said in the Walkie-Talkie message. Steve answered, "Phil has gold in his hand, and he's telling me, 'Okay, you've got to do this to beat me.'"

During the medal ceremony, the strains of the "Star Spangled Banner" crackled in the frigid air as two American flags flapped in the breeze. The Mahre twins stood on the victory stand, silver and gold around their necks, showing the world a double win in more ways than one.[3]

Later in 1984 at the summer games, Mike Conley, America's best triple jumper, sprained his ankle on his first try and later finished second to Al Joyner by a scant three inches. Joyner won the gold, Conley had to settle for the silver. Believers in win/lose thinking were sure it was a tragedy, but not Conley. He didn't stick his silver medal away in some drawer and lament to anyone who would listen about his great misfortune. Instead, he began showing up at other track meets dressed entirely in silver. His shoes were silver, his uniform was silver and he even brought his silver medal.[4]

Was Conley just trying to make the best out of having to dine on sour grapes? Not necessarily. Perhaps he'd read the writing of a philosopher named Cicero, who said in 55 B.C., "If you aspire to the highest place, it is no disgrace to stop at the second, or even the third."

Or, Conley could have turned to the New Testament, which puts all greedy scrambling for first place in proper perspective. Jesus, for example, taught His disciples not to take the place of honor, but to wait until they were assigned their seats. In fact, they were to take the lowest place and wait for the host to invite them to move up higher. And, He capped His teaching by saying, "Everyone who exalts himself will be humbled, and he who humbles himself will be exalted" (Luke 14:11).

Unfortunately, the world competes on the basis of self-exaltation. You can find all kinds of materials to teach you the mental gymnastics necessary to win "the power game." There are all kinds of ways to exalt yourself around the office and try to ace out people who are competing with you for a better position. But if you want to enjoy the tension of being a Christian in a competitive, secular world, keep in mind how Paul echoed Jesus' teachings about self-exaltation. Paul loved athletics and even wrote of disciplining his body so he would not run aimlessly in quest of "the prize" (see 1 Cor. 9:24-27).

But Paul also wrote about not thinking of yourself more highly than you ought and doing nothing out of selfishness or conceit, being humble and regarding others as more important than yourself (see Rom. 12:3 and Phil. 2:3).

Writing in *Eternity* magazine, Nancy Barcus had this to say about winning by cooperation instead of engaging in cutthroat competition.

> Rather than feeling we must "seize opportunity all at once," a Christian is more likely to think of life as a pilgrimage or an unfolding book, and that from day to day God is working out this perfect plan within us. Good things take time. Those who rush ahead of us may gain opportunities they are as yet ill-suited to perform. When our turn comes, we want to be ready. Meanwhile, we learn the spiritual lesson of patience—letting God work in His own time.[5]

To put it another way, you can seek your own kingdom or you can seek the one Jesus continually talked about. If you're seeking your own kingdom, tooth-and-claw competition will come naturally. Your killer instinct may take you to the top of the heap. If you seek Christ's kingdom, you will probably have to start at the bottom and the tooth-and-claw types may step on your face as they climb to the summit.

As the unknown bumper sticker philosopher observes: "I was winning the rat race and then along came faster rats." In one sense he is right; there are a lot of faster rats out there. But winning the rat race and a crown that will fade is not what it's really all about. Following Christ turns the rat race into a glorious marathon. And waiting at the finish line is a crown that will last forever.

Lord, help me remember that You did not create the rat race; men do as they try to claw their way up. Help me run Your race, for Your glory, and show me how I can help others as well.

———————

How competitive are you? Are there any areas of life where you want to win too much? If so, why? Have you ever been in a situation similar to Steve and Phil Mahre, where you actually tried to help someone else do the best he could to win—even at your expense? If you ever were in such a situation, what would you do?

Notes
1. Denis Waitley, *The Double Win* (Old Tappan: Fleming H. Revell, 1985), p. 32.
2. Donald V. Seibert and William Proctor, *The Ethical Executive* (New York: Cornerstone Library, A Division of Simon & Schuster, 1984), pp. 20,21.
3. Denis Waitley tells this story in *The Double Win*, pp. 42-43. Quotes by the Mahre twins were taken from a report in the *New York Times*, February 20, 1984, p. C6.
4. See Jim Murray, "A Second Opinion on Being First," *Los Angeles Times*, Friday, March 8, 1985.
5. Nancy Barcus, "Winning by Cooperation," *Eternity*, September 1983, p. 63.

CHAPTER TEN

But You Can't Eat Treasures in Heaven—or Can You?

"The point is, ladies and gentlemen, greed, for lack of a better word, is good. Greed is right. Greed works. Greed clarifies, cuts through and captures the essence of the evolutionary spirit."

—From a speech to the stockholders by corporate raider Gordon Gekko, in the film *Wall Street*

"Whoever loves money never has money enough."

—Ecclesiastes 5:10

The ever-entrepreneurial film industry always reflects the present culture, and in 1987 *Wall Street* opened just before Christmas. The movie starred Charlie Sheen as Bud Fox, an ambitious young broker, and Michael Douglas as Gordon Gekko, a high-rolling, corporate raider, who took Fox under his wing to teach him the business (i.e., how to cheat). When Fox finally saw the light and confronted Gekko about his back-stabbing ways, Gekko replied glibly, "It's all about bucks, Kid. The rest is conversation!"

Grasping for big bucks in the '80s produced the Yuppie phenomenon—the young urban professionals who couldn't make or spend money fast enough. The lust for lucre was everywhere, from inside traders like Ivan Boesky to televangelists Jim and Tammy Bakker, whose well-publicized excesses included gold plumbing fixtures and an air-conditioned doghouse. Boesky and Bakker, by the way, both wound up in prison.

As we moved into the '90s, there was a backlash that seemed to put greed out of style. People began realizing that riches are no substitute for relationships. Some observers believe the backlash started when the stock market took its heady plunge in October, 1987. Marketing consultant Faith Popcorn coined the term "Yuppie glut" and predicted a new trend, known as "cashing out," which would involve turning down promotions, longer hours and extended business trips in order to devote more time to family, friends and community.[1]

It's almost as though secular society had eavesdropped on the pastors who were still valiantly trying to remind their flocks of the words of Jesus:

> Do not store up for yourselves treasures on earth, where moth and rust destroy, and where thieves break in and steal. But store up for your-

selves treasures in heaven, where moth and rust do not destroy, and where thieves do not break in and steal. For where your treasure is, there your heart will be also (Matt. 6:19-21).

Jesus didn't utter these words at a meeting of the Palestinian chapter of the Billionaire Boys Club. While He did tell one of the Donald Trumps of His day that it was easier for a camel to go through the eye of the needle than for a rich man to enter God's kingdom (see Matt. 19:24), He saved His most potent remarks on materialism and greed for just plain churchgoers like you and me.

Most of those listening to the Sermon on the Mount were common people, who had to scramble and scrape just to get by. Any one of them might have responded, "Rabbi, that's all very good, but how do I eat treasures in heaven? I've got kids to feed and a mortgage to pay. Save these worries about treasures on earth for the ones who have some treasures!"

Today many Christian believers might echo that kind of protest. "Materialism and greed? With both of us working, we're barely getting by. We couldn't afford seven dollar tickets to see Wall Street and our doghouse isn't air conditioned. Come to think of it, at the moment, our home isn't air conditioned, and it's going to cost eight hundred bucks to fix something called a compressor."

To which Jesus might answer, "Do you think you have to be rich to be greedy or materialistic? Look around you. Better yet, look inside."

If Jesus thought the average, middle-class folk of His day needed to hear about treasures in heaven versus treasures on earth, what about us? Randy Alcorn, author of *Money, Possessions and Eternity*, writes:

The hardest part of dealing with our materialism is that it has become so much a part of us. Like people who have lived in darkness for years, we have been removed from the light so long we do not know how dark it really is. Many of us have never known what it is not to be materialistic. It is normal, the only way we know.[2]

Alcorn's words bring to mind the fish that live at the bottom of the ocean at depths so great no light ever penetrates that far down. These fish have no eyes because they don't need them in the pitch blackness. In our case, however, we're swimming in a sea of materialism where there is plenty of light, and that's just the problem. The world is full of things that cause "the lust of his eyes" (see 1 John 2:16), and we need to gain a clearer vision of the difference between treasures in heaven and treasures on earth.

Jesus knew that His listeners (and we who would follow) would need some help with their vision. That's why He went on to say:

The eye is the lamp of the body. If your eyes are good, your whole body will be full of light. But if your eyes are bad, your whole body will be full of darkness. If then the light within you is darkness, how great is that darkness! (Matt. 6:22,23).

You may have heard the expression, "The eyes are the windows of the soul." What Jesus is saying is that, just as windows admit light into a room, your eyes admit light into your heart and soul. If the windows to a room are dirty, little light can get through; the same is true with a person's eyes. If there is something clouding your vision, your soul will live in shadows.

The Greek word "good" in verse 22 actually means generous or liberal. The word "bad" in verse 23 can be translated niggardly or grudging. What Jesus is helping us think about is how generous or how grasping and greedy we might be. The person with a generous eye will find God's light flooding his soul, while a person with a grasp-

---

The person with a generous eye will find God's light flooding his soul, while a person with a grasping or greedy eye will live in darkness.

---

ing or greedy eye will live in darkness. And, as Jesus said, "How great is that darkness!"

Jesus reminds us that materialism—the concept that the physical is only what is real and important—is the very antithesis of the Christian life. The trouble is, it is so easy to see the material—the flash, the glitter, the glamour of the good life. To see the spiritual, we need clear eyes of faith that can discern the folly in bumper stickers like: "HE WHO DIES WITH THE MOST TOYS WINS."

John D. Rockefeller was one of the wealthiest men in history, and when he died someone asked his accountant, "How much did John D. leave?"

The accountant's reply: "He left all of it."

Laying up treasures on earth may give temporary satisfaction but you always leave it all behind. On the other hand, laying up treasures in heaven means you can "take it with you," because it's already there.

Lord, give my soul twenty-twenty vision. Help me look past the clutter of things to where life is supposed to lead.

Sit down with your spouse (and/or your children) and discuss the difference between laying up treasures on earth and treasures in heaven. What specific steps can you take to be aware of and neutralize the materialism and consumerism that engulfs your family daily? Perhaps a first step is as simple as spending less on yourselves and more on God's work. But is that the first step? Is there something even more basic?

Notes
1. See Brownstein and Easton, "The Status Seekers," *Los Angeles Times Magazine.*
2. Randy Alcorn, Money, Possessions and Eternity (Wheaton: Tyndale House Publishers, Inc., 1989), p. 60.

CHAPTER ELEVEN

How Much Is Enough?

Money isn't everything, but it's
right up there with air
and water.[1]

"Though your riches increase, do
not set your heart on them."
—Psalm 62:10

The atheist Voltaire once said, "When it is a question of money, everybody is of the same religion."

Voltaire's remark reminds me of another comment I heard from a colleague with whom I worked for many years at Gospel Light Publications, one of the leading publishers of Sunday School curriculum in America. Dr. Milford Sholund is a Swedish combination of pastor, theologian, humorist and country-style philosopher. At GL we called him "Moses" because it was his job to lay down the law and get all of us to meet our deadlines. One day, after discussing the costs of a particular project and how we could develop a quality product at a price low enough for most churches to use, Milford paused and, with a twinkle in his eye, said, "Well, just remember, money is god!"

He was joking, of course, but behind his cracker barrel hyperbole was a great insight on our human condition, whether we are in the Kingdom, outside or just looking. Our fervent claims of devotion and worship notwithstanding, we often find ourselves realizing that once again money has become so important that God is in grave danger of being ignored or, worse, patronized.

But God will not be treated condescendingly. It's not surprising that Jesus, after telling His listeners on the mountainside to lay up treasures in heaven rather than on earth and to keep their vision clear of the clutter of materialism, went on to say, "No one can serve two masters. Either he will hate the one and love the other, or he will be devoted to the one and despise the other. You cannot serve both God and Money" (Matt. 6:24).

One of the beautiful things about Jesus' teaching is that it is so brief and succinct. He cuts right through all the possible ways we might try to relax our standards and gets down to the bottom line, saying, "You can't serve God and money." Older translations of the Bible used the word "mammon," a Hebrew word meaning material possessions. In times past, people entrusted their mammon to others, just as we entrust money to a bank today. But in Jesus' day Mammon had come to mean "something in which people put their trust" and it was spelled with a capital *M*. Jesus' listeners knew exactly what He was talking about: Mammon had become a god and He was telling them they must choose between the real God and a lesser one.[2]

In commenting on this verse, William Barclay points out that the word "serve" actually means "be a slave to," and the word "master" denotes "absolute ownership." Barclay believes it would be more accurate to translate the verse: "No man can be a slave to two owners."[3]

Suddenly this verse starts becoming uncomfortable, indeed. In our modern civilized Western world, slavery has supposedly been condemned and abolished. One of the main planks in the platform of the American dream is that every man, woman and child is free to do, be and say just about anything, as long as we break no laws and harm nobody else. Down through the centuries, however, slaves were literally living tools, who had no time that was their own. They had to account to their masters for every second of their lives.

Such a concept is totally foreign to us today. True, we have our jobs and our equivalent of a "master" who is our boss, our employer or perhaps "the corporation." But unless we are driven by workaholism or some other addiction, we are not slaves who have no power over what happens to us. Many people find that their real interests lie in their leisure activities, their hobbies, or even in a second job or avocation during their off-hours each week. But in the ancient world, and even on the plantations of the Southern states in the nineteenth century, slaves had no hobbies, no second jobs and very little leisure. If they "moonlighted," it simply meant working past sundown for their masters to get whatever needed doing done.

Uncomfortable as it may sound, Jesus is saying we have no rights of our own. God is our undisputed Master. He does not share this position with anyone in any way. Theoretically, Christians never ask, "What do I want to do?" We are supposed to ask, "What does God want me to do?" As William Barclay writes, Christians have "no time off from being a Christian....A partial or a spasmodic service of God is not enough. Being a Christian is a whole-time job."[4]

It's easy to read the words, "You cannot serve both God and money," and attest, "Yes, those are my Christian sentiments exactly." But living in a consumer culture lures us into serving two masters anyway.

Credit cards weren't around when Jesus preached the Sermon on the Mount, but His warning about money is timeless. One of the signs of our times is the "consumer credit counselor" who advises people who have plunged so deep into debt with credit cards that they face total financial despair and disaster. According to one of these counselors, the people who get into the most trouble are usually young adults in their 20s and 30s.

Take for example a 35-year-old financial adviser who earns $50,000 a year and who is $50,000 in debt.[5] That $50,000 includes $10,000 on charge cards, $30,000 for student loans and $10,000 loaned to him by his father to help him get his education.

How did he get into this mess? For starters, he admits that he "likes nice things." When tempted to buy a new TV, microwave or stereo, he often succumbs, thinking that he is so deeply in debt already a few more dollars won't make that much difference. In addition, he took a year off from his job to earn a higher graduate degree, putting living expenses on charge cards. He wound up making monthly payments of $350 on student loans, $300 on credit cards, $100 to his father, $700 rent and $80 for the minimum car insurance he needs in order to drive.

After paying all these bills, this man is left with less

Prosperity theology and the gospel of "name it and claim it" have tempted many believers into spending more than they earn and giving very little back to the Lord.

---

than $500 a month for utilities, food, gas and clothing, which includes $300 suits that he wears to his job with a large corporation where, ironically, he advises others on how to handle their finances! He freely admits that he pays his debts with one hand and charges with the other. Savings are out of the question, but he is hardly alone in that regard. In the mid-1970s across America, the personal savings rate (percentage of after tax income saved) was around 9 percent. By 1987, it dipped to 3.7 percent, and by 1988 it managed to crawl back up to 4.9 percent.[6]
One reason our personal savings rate is so low is that consumerism is encouraged on every hand to keep the U. S. economy rolling. Consider this interesting statistic: consumer spending accounts for two-thirds of the $5.4 trillion U.S. economy. No wonder Americans are encouraged to spend beyond their means, to get what they want now and make monthly payments later.

But, people can get out of debt and stay out of debt—if

they want to. In one case, a physical education teacher came to a credit counselor's office with $42,000 in credit card bills. Within two years he had reduced that debt to $17,000, and expected to have it fully under control in another year. This teacher, who earned around $40,000 a year, used to charge everything from limousine rides to a Lear jet trip to Las Vegas, which cost him $3,000. But once he became "anti-plastic," he made a new rule: "If I can't pay cash or put it on layaway, I don't need it."[7]

No information is available on whether or not any of the people in the above examples are Christians, but it's certainly possible. Prosperity theology and the gospel of "name it and claim it" have tempted many believers into spending more than they earn and giving very little back to the Lord.

But suppose all the Christians in the United States alone were out of debt? How many millions of dollars would be freed up for the work of the Kingdom? Obviously, all the Christians aren't out of debt. In fact, millions of them are up to their armpits in mortgages and credit card bills. Instead of being slaves to God, they are slaves to a monthly credit card statement. Solomon, one of the world's richest men, put it well: "The rich rule over the poor, and the borrower is servant to the lender" (Prov. 22:7).

Scripture teaches that God has lent us His creation, and that we are responsible for being good stewards. How much better to live under His rule and be His servants, instead of being slaves to Mammon. Besides, the interest rates are a lot lower!

———————

Lord, You know I love you. Help me hate any habit, particularly a spending habit, that undermines that love.

———————

An old adage suggests that we divide our income as follows: Give ten percent, save ten percent, and live on the rest. How close are you coming to that rule of thumb? Or does it seem totally unrealistic?

Some basic questions to consider before you go into debt or increase the debts you already have:

- Is this something I need or something I want?
- Does God want me to have this, or am I simply presuming that He will help me pay for it?
- Is buying this going to help me uphold my convictions as a Christian?
- By going into debt (or further into debt), am I being tempted to rob God? In other words, will I wind up having to pay my creditors first and God second, or possibly not at all?
- Do my debts prevent me from reaching out to help others when the Holy Spirit makes it clear there is an opportunity to do so?

Notes
1. Author unknown. Seen on a bumper sticker.
2. William Barclay, *The Daily Study Bible, Gospel of Matthew,* Volume 1 (Edinburgh: The St. Andrew Press, 1956), p. 252.
3. Ibid., see p. 252.
4. Ibid., see p. 252.
5. See Jennifer Lowe, "Come On, Give Me Some Credit," *Daily News,* Sunday, January 24, 1988, L.A. Life Section, p. 5.
6. Statistics according to the International Monetary Fund, quoted by Marcy Eckroth Mullins, USA *Today,* May 16, 1988, p. 1B.
7. Jennifer Lowe, "Come On, Give Me Some Credit," *Daily News,* Sunday, January 24, 1988, L.A. Life Section, p. 5.

CHAPTER TWELVE

You Can't Save Room for Dessert When You Eat It First

"I think [my] closet has inside at least, at least, a million dollars' worth of clothes, the furs included. But, girls, I work very hard. No man ever gave me a penny, as a matter of fact. So why shall I not spend on myself?"

—Zsa Zsa Gabor[1]

"Whoever trusts in his riches will fall."

—Proverbs 11:28

One way I can measure my treasures on earth against my treasures in heaven is to check to see how often I play the "if only—then" game. The rules are simple. All I need to do is think of all the things I believe I need to make me happy and I'm off and running:

- *If only* I can get that promotion...*then* I'll get some respect around here.
- *If only* we can both keep working just a few more years...then we'll be able to slow down.
- *If only* I could buy her that diamond anniversary band...then she'll know how much I love her.
- *If only* we could afford to build that mountain cabin...then we'd always have great weekends and vacations.

It's funny how the "if only—then" game often involves money. To paraphrase Tevye in *Fiddler on the Roof*: "*If only* I were a rich man...*then* I could biddy biddy bum all day long!" Or, as a poster I found in a print shop puts it:

LIFE IS UNCERTAIN...
EAT DESSERT FIRST!

But "Lifestyles of the Rich and Famous" notwithstanding, the rich don't always get to eat dessert first and biddy biddy bum all day long.

William H. Vanderbilt complained that the care of two hundred million dollars was "enough to kill anyone. There is no pleasure in it." Many other fabulously rich men have made similar observations, including Andrew Carnegie, the well-known philanthropist, who gave the world a possible clue about the reason for his generosity when he said, "Millionaires seldom smile."

Despite all the rumors, money does not come with a

lifetime happiness guarantee. In fact, according to one psychiatric study, it guarantees that you can become a major suicide risk. One of the fifteen major contributors to a suicidal frame of mind is "having financial resources." The study revealed, the more a man has the more he may be tempted to think about killing himself.[2]

It's even becoming risky to own nice things to wear. On a spring day in 1989 a fifteen-year-old boy left home for school, proudly wearing a badge of affluence that would make him the envy, or at least the equal, of all he met—a new pair of Air Jordan athletic shoes, costing one hundred dollars. The next day the boy's body was found in a field not far from his school, and a seventeen-year-old was arrested for his murder. When picked up, the seventeen-year-old had on the Air Jordans. He had killed in order to get them.[3]

A rare and isolated case, you say? Not really. The fifteen-year-old boy who died because he chose to wear expensive shoes was the third victim to be killed for his clothing during a five-year period in his community. And while murder is an infrequent extreme, being robbed for your clothes isn't. Across the nation kids are being relieved daily of name brand sneakers, designer jogging suits, leather jackets and jewelry.

School officials, psychologists, school board members—and even the children themselves agree that having the right thing to wear, the top brand name on your hip pocket, has become practically imperative. The phrase often used is "clothes fixated." Worried that what they wear will not be "in" and they'll be "out" of the peer group, children pressure their overindulgent parents to buy them the best of the brand names. The old saying used to have it, "Clothes make the man." Today, clothes make the four-year-old and on up.[4]

The president of a large advertising agency who handles accounts for a number of children's clothing lines admits that as a mother she's concerned about what advertising can do to the minds of young people. Nancy Shalek says, "Advertising at its best is making people feel that without their product, you're a loser. Kids are very

---

It's high time we quit playing designer/ dessert games while dancing to Fifth Avenue's catchy little tunes.

---

sensitive to that. If you tell them to buy something, they are resistant. But if you tell them they'll be a dork if they don't, you've got their attention."[5]

To show up not wearing Nike, Reebok, Jordache, Guess and dozens of other brand names, is to risk ridicule, scorn and even ostracism by your classmates. As one ten-year-old put it: "People will tease you and talk about you, say you got on no-name shoes or say you shop at K Mart."[6]

The cause of this kind of cruelty is a potent combination of the power of advertising with peer group pressure. The designer label means everything because it's the way of letting everyone else know that you have "high value." Ask a typical student if she or he would wear expensive name brand clothes or shoes without a designer label, and he or she would say no. Why? Simple. Without the label, nobody would know what it costs. Quality and long wear aren't really the issue; status and elitism are what count.

What makes parents give in to the demands of children who just have to have the most of the best at any price? Is it covetousness, envy and greed? These forces are undoubtedly at work, but what about fear, anxiety and low self-esteem? As Randy Alcorn points out, "The uncertainty and insecurity of material things makes materialism the mother of anxiety."[7]

It is no surprise, then, that Jesus follows up His challenge to lay up treasures in heaven and serve only one Master—God—with some comments about how unnecessary it is to eat dessert first while attired in designer labels:

> Therefore I tell you, do not worry about your life, what you will eat or drink; or about your body, what you will wear. Is not life more important than food, and the body more important than clothes? Look at the birds of the air; they do not sow or reap or store away in barns, and yet your heavenly Father feeds them. Are you not much more valuable than they? Who of you by worrying can add a single hour to his life?
>
> And why do you worry about clothes? See how the lilies of the field grow. They do not labor or spin. Yet I tell you that not even Solomon in all his splendor was dressed like one of these. If that is how God clothes the grass of the field, which is here today and tomorrow is thrown into the fire, will He not much more clothe you, O you of little faith? So do not worry, saying, "What shall we eat?" or "What shall we drink?" or "What shall we wear?" For the pagans run after all these things, and your heavenly Father knows that you need them. But seek first his kingdom and his righteousness, and all these things will be given to you as well. Therefore do not worry about tomorrow, for

tomorrow will worry about itself. Each day has enough trouble of its own (Matt. 6:25-34).

Jesus isn't saying, "Kick back and flake out." Instead, He is saying, "Don't be so full of care. Don't let worries over gaining status, esteem and security take all the joy out of living."

Those who join the rat race to the latest sale of designer label shoes or clothes are missing the real joy in life for several reasons. They're forgetting that life is more than what you eat or wear. Worrying about what you need (not to mention what you want) is as pointless as wishing you were two inches taller.

Worrying says you distrust God, and appear to have no more resources than the pagans (those who don't know Christ). Jesus isn't referring to savages in loin cloths; He is talking about nicely dressed, sophisticated, well-educated folk—the kind that live on your block. Some of the nicest people you may be trying to impress are pagans. As someone said, "One reason why it's hard to save money is that our neighbors are always buying something we can't afford."[8]

And that's just the point. It's high time we quit playing designer/dessert games while dancing to Fifth Avenue's catchy little tunes. Granted, this won't be easy. Parents, especially, will have to "suck it up" and figure out how to make a stand when the kids charge at them demanding another designer label because "all the other kids have one." Each family will have to decide where to draw the line. But just imagine how it would spice up family discussions to sit down and figure out together where that line is and what wearing designer clothes really has to do with what Jesus is all about.

Everyone may be pleasantly surprised. The kids will

learn that they don't necessarily have to shop in thrift stores, but parents can get across their point as well: Turning life into one big dessert buffet because everybody else seems to be doing it is not the way your family wants to live.

But how, specifically, can we draw the line on designer-label living?

We can concentrate on being part of God's kingdom instead of a cog in the world's materialistic machine. Every believer is in the Kingdom, but it's easy to let one foot stray into the other camp—and often it's the foot adorned with exorbitantly priced designer labels. In the prayer He taught His disciples, Jesus included the phrase, "Thy kingdom come. Thy will be done" (see Matt. 6:10, *KJV*). Clearly, Jesus is saying that if we are in the Kingdom, we will want to do God's will. And the more we concentrate on doing God's will, the easier it will be to resist those pressures that ask us to spend more and more to enjoy less and less.

We can focus on God's approval rather than on the approval of others for our sense of well-being. The entire sixty-second Psalm tells us that our honor and salvation depend on God alone. God surely is concerned with what we wear, and He provides "garments of salvation" and "a robe of righteousness" (see Isa. 61:10). How ironic that we focus more on the kind of garments that we think will endear us to our friends, or to the in-group.

Seeking first God's kingdom doesn't mean we can never have dessert. It doesn't mean that we have to dress "hopelessly out of fashion." But when we seek first the kingdom of God, we are not slaves to fashion or other manipulations of the System. We won't have to experience the poverty that comes from having too much.

For example, poverty can be having a closet full of

clothes and wailing, "I haven't got a thing to wear." Poverty can be eating so often you are forced to choose between Diet Center and Jenny Craig. Poverty can mean having a college education, a good salary, perks galore— and not really enjoying what you do. In short, poverty can be a bigger problem for your soul than it can be for your body.[9]

"Dessert first living" always leads to poverty; Kingdom first living leads to true wealth.

Lord, I want to seek your Kingdom first, but it's easy to get confused. Help me filter out all the hype, lies and video tape so I can see Your will, which has already been clearly spelled out in Scripture.

In what ways is your family "seeking first the kingdom of God"? What pressures are tempting you to seek other things first? How serious is designer label anxiety at your house?

Talk with your spouse and/or your children about the implications in believing the philosophy behind "Life is uncertain...eat dessert first."

Notes
1. Ms. Gabor made this statement while appearing as a guest on "The Oprah Winfrey Show," No. 565, "Tours of Shopaholics' Closets," air date November 11, 1988.
2. See Randy Alcorn, *Money, Possessions and Eternity* (Wheaton: Tyndale House Publishers, Inc., 1989), p. 69.
3. See Ron Harris, "Children Who Dress for Excess," *Los Angeles Times*, Sunday, November 12, 1989, p. A1.
4. Ibid., p. A26.
5. Ibid.
6. Ibid.
7. Randy Alcorn, *Money, Possessions and Eternity*, p. 69.
8. Quoted by Eleanor Doan, *Speaker's Source Book* (Grand Rapids: Zondervan Publishing House, 1960), p. 167.
9. Adapted from Denis Waitley, *Being the Best* (Nashville: Oliver Nelson, 1987), p. 96.

CHAPTER THIRTEEN

Is Self-fulfillment Good or Bad?

There once was a nymph
named Narcissus
Who thought himself very
delicious;
So he stared like a fool
At his face in a pool,
And his folly today is still
with us.[1]

"My soul thirsts for God, for
the living God."
—Psalm 42:2

What makes all of us run? Why do we get caught up in schedules that are pressed down, shaken together and running over, with to-do lists that would leave Superman panting? Why do we wind up with so many commitments that life—at least at times—does turn into a rat race, seemingly mindless scampering around and around on a little wheel? We are busy, but we wonder: *Are we making any progress?*

There are all sorts of explanations for our busy-ness. We may be trying to show a disapproving parent we really can do it all after all. Perhaps we are perfectionists with a penchant for biting off more than we can chew, and then pressing the panic button when there isn't time to "do it right" (see chapter 18). Maybe we have an overdeveloped sense of responsibility, always aware of all that needs to be done—all those people out there who need help.

These explanations, and others like them, only nibble at a larger truth. The real cause of why we run so fast and so far lies deeper. In the bedrock of our personalities is the need to feel that life is worth it, that who we are and what we do is meaningful.

In recent years, literally tons of literature have been written on self-esteem and self-image, some good, some bad. But just about all of it has found a ready market for one reason: people need to feel good about themselves. If your self-image is high, strong and healthy, life looks much brighter and you feel that just about anything is possible. If your self-image is low, life looks gray, bleak and even hopeless.

Lack of a good self-image may not be the major problem plaguing mankind, but it's right up there with plaque and nuclear war. Lack of a good self-image hampers—and even cripples—millions, but where do Christians fit into the self-image issue?

As the 1990s began, the average believer could turn to one of two loud voices in the Christian camp. On the left, they could hear that self-esteem is the God-given right of every Christian and that they can have it through a positive mental attitude, possibility thinking, and "unleashing the giant within them." On the right, they would hear, however, that any talk of self-esteem is a contradiction for a Christian. In fact, the Bible says nothing about self-acceptance, self-love, self-assertion, self-confidence, self-forgiveness or self-esteem. To think of self is a no-no and something no self-respecting (whoops!) Christian would ever do.

Writing in *Christianity Today,* John Stott points to the Cross itself as the middle ground between self-love and self-denial. Because the pressures and pains of living dehumanize people and make them feel worthless, demeaned, and like failures, Stott asks the question that every Christian would like answered: "Am I supposed to love myself or hate myself?"

He emphatically rejects the idea that Jesus commanded self-love when He repeated Moses' command to "Love your neighbor as yourself." Grammatically, all that Jesus meant was that most people already are looking out for themselves quite well and that they should at least try doing it for their neighbors, too. In addition, Jesus was speaking of agape love—self-sacrifice to help and serve others. It would be difficult to love yourself by means of self-sacrifice. Third, Stott points out that self-love is what the Bible calls sin. He mentions Paul's words: in the last days, people will be lovers of self instead of lovers of God (see 2 Tim. 3:1-4).[2]

All this makes sense, but if self-love is bad, does that make self-hatred good? When Paul says in Romans 12:3, for example, "Do not think of yourself more highly than you ought," is he saying that you shouldn't think of yourself positively at all?

There is plenty of evidence in Scripture that seems to point to the idea that we must do away with the self completely. Jesus clearly called us to self-denial when He said, "If anyone would come after me, he must deny himself and take up his cross and follow me" (Matt. 16:24).

Stott points out that Jesus' disciples knew exactly what He meant by "taking up the cross." People carrying their own crosses to their scene of execution were a common sight throughout Palestine. Eventually, Jesus had to do the same thing. Jesus uses vivid imagery to tell His disciples that following Him means denying yourself, killing something inside that will come between you and Him.

Some people put "self-denial" in the category of giving up something for Lent, dieting or trying to stop smoking. The kind of self-denial Jesus is talking about goes much deeper. You have to deny your supposed right to go your own way. As the apostle Paul put it, you have to crucify your sinful nature with its passions and desires (see Gal. 5:24).

So far, it sounds bad for the self or having any concept of self. But as Stott points out, along with his call to self-denial, Jesus also called us to self-affirmation. Not self-love, but self-affirmation. For example, as we saw in the last chapter, when Jesus advised the crowds not to worry about what they ate or what they wore, He clearly said that they were much more valuable than the birds of the air.

What gives us our value? We are made in God's image, and, as a young black man once said when fed up with the frustrations of living in a racist society, "I'm me and I'm good, 'cos God don't make junk!'"

Jesus not only said people are valuable, He treated them that way. He "loved everybody" (although He was a bit hard on the Pharisees for their own good). He was the friend of publicans, sinners, the diseased, the poor, the hungry, the outcasts. He was put down for associating with this "kind" of person, but He made it clear that He valued and loved them anyway.

The critics of selfism are partly right, but after they blast away at terms like self-esteem, self-image and self-love, we are left feeling we must deny being selves of any kind. Yet each of us is a self, an individual person, made in God's image.

He also valued and loved the rich folk, but made it clear that some of them had to do some changing. The rich young ruler couldn't change and went away sorrowful (see Luke 18:18-24). Zacchaeus, the rich tax collector, did change and came away with infinitely more than he could ever have known through the riches he had gained by theft and treachery (see Luke 19:1-9).

Jesus' final act of showing how much we are worth was His sacrifice on the Cross. He gave His life as a ransom for many "selves" like you and me. He didn't give His life for non-entities or non-selves. He laid down His life for the sheep, and each one of those "sheep" is a self.

So, we seem to be faced with a problem. How can we deny and crucify ourselves, yet affirm and value ourselves, as well?

John Stott resolves the paradox by defining "self" as a "complex entity of good and evil, glory and shame."[3] In other words, part of your "self" is the result of God's creation because you are made in His image. But another part of your self is the result of the Fall, which defaced and cracked that image. When Jesus calls us to deny ourselves, He is referring to the fallen self that is concerned only with its own agenda. That self needs crucifying and burying, but not resurrecting. Stott puts it in a nutshell when he adds:

> There is, therefore, a great need for discernment in our self-understanding. Who am I? What is my "self"? The answer: I'm a Jeckyl and Hyde, a mixed-up kid, having both dignity, because I was created in God's image, and depravity, because I am fallen and rebellious. I am both noble and ignoble, beautiful and ugly, good and bad, upright and twisted, image of God and slave of the devil. My true self is what I am by creation, which Christ came to redeem. My fallen self is what I am by the fall, which Christ came to destroy.[4]

Or, to use Paul's words to the Ephesians: "You were taught, with regard to your former way of life, to put off your old self, which is being corrupted by its deceitful desires; to be made new in the attitude of your minds; and to put on the new self, created to be like God in true righteousness and holiness" (Eph. 4:22-24).

Coming back to the question, "Is self-fulfillment good or bad?" we must first ask which self do we want to fulfill? The old fallen self, which is always ready for another ego trip into self-centeredness and all the other personifications of self-love gone to seed? Or, the new self, redeemed by Christ with the opportunity and power to be like God?

The critics of selfism are partly right, but after they blast away at terms like self-esteem, self-image and self-love, we are left feeling we must deny being selves of any kind. We wonder if being a Christian means being a zero with the center rubbed out. Yet each of us is a self, an individual person, made in God's image. That image was marred by the Fall, and before coming to Christ a person can only pursue selfishness because he or she has no other option. After coming to Christ, there is a choice. Instead of self-centeredness, we can choose self-denial. Instead of self-indulgence, we can choose self-control.

Amazingly, we are free to choose one or the other, and if we make the wrong choices, we will have to live on the periphery of all God has for us. But if we make the right choices and draw closer to the Center, we will know what Jesus meant when He said, "I have come that they may have life, and have it to the full" (John 10:10).

It is quite clear that the road to selfism can become the same road where they hold the rat race. True self-fulfillment, however, is running another kind of race described by the writer of Hebrews who suggests that we keep our eyes fixed on Jesus, the Author and Finisher of our faith (see Heb. 12:1,2). Then our "new selves" will be filled full, not by us, but by the Lord of heaven.

Lord, help me put my old self to death. Fulfill my new self,
as only You can.

Think back over the past six to twelve months. How "fulfilling" has this time been for you? What connections do you see between feeling fulfilled and being made new in the attitude of your mind, putting on the new self, created to be like God in true righteousness and holiness? (See Eph. 4:22-24.)

Notes
1. Quoted by John R.W. Stott, "Am I Supposed to Love Myself or Hate Myself?" *Christianity Today*, April 20, 1984, p. 26, original source unknown.
2. John R. W. Stott, "Am I supposed to Love Myself or Hate Myself?" *Christianity Today*, April 20, 1984, p. 26.
3. John Stott, *Christianity Today*, p. 28.
4. Ibid p. 28.

CHAPTER FOURTEEN

It's a Jungle Out There, Especially for Grasshoppers

"When you're born, you're taking a big chance."
—Ashleigh Brilliant[1]

"What is man that you are mindful of him?"
—Psalm 8:4

It's all very well to discover that it's okay to develop a healthy self-image through letting God do the fulfilling of your life, but what if you don't feel there is much of a "self" for Him to work with? Scripture warns us repeatedly against thinking of ourselves more highly than we ought to think (see Rom. 12:3; Phil. 2:3,4), but what about thinking of yourself *too lowly*?

Counselors' offices are full of people with inferiority complexes, and many of them are Christians who might ruefully agree with the bumper sticker that quips:

JUST BECAUSE YOU'RE PARANOID
DOESN'T MEAN THEY'RE NOT OUT TO GET YOU.

If everyone who comes to Christ is a new creation (see 2 Cor. 5:17), transformed from the kingdom of darkness to the kingdom of light (see Col. 1:12,13), why all this inferiority, fear and failure? Why do songs like "Victory in Jesus" taste like ashes in the mouths of so many of the faithful?

To add to their pain, these people are often told that their feelings are the result of some "secret sin," or at least "a lack of faith." But that doesn't take away the pain of a low self-concept; in fact, it usually only increases it. As a well-known song by the Beatles suggests, the person with a low self-image winds up in nowhere land, making nowhere plans for nobody.[2]

Twenty years ago, Dorothy Corkille Briggs said in her classic book, *Your Child's Self-Esteem*:

High self-esteem is not a noisy conceit. It is a quiet sense of self-respect, a feeling of self-worth. When you have it deep inside, you're glad you're you. Conceit is but whitewash to cover low self-esteem. With high self-esteem, you don't waste time and energy impressing others; you already know you have value.[3]

From the mouth of a secular expert on child rearing comes an apt description of what it should be like to be a child of God. Yet, many children of God struggle with low self-esteem and often try to hide it behind a mask of "pious humility."

Most counselors are agreed that low self-esteem begins in childhood. We may enter this world as a blank page, but people soon start marking all over it and the typical result is not a pretty picture. James Dobson, founder and director of Focus on the Family, writes:

> The current epidemic of self-doubt has resulted from a totally unjust and unnecessary system of evaluating human worth, now prevalent in our society. Not everyone is seen as worthy; not everyone is accepted. Instead, we reserve our praise and admiration for a select few who have been blessed from birth with the characteristics we value most highly. It is a vicious system, and we, as parents, must counterbalance its impact.[4]

Guided by experts like Dobson and Briggs, parents of the last generation or two have been working on building healthy self-esteem in their children, but with limited success. The current drug crisis is a major evidence of a lack of self-esteem among the young. One reason parents are having trouble transmitting high self-esteem to their children is that they don't have high self-esteem themselves.

The typical mom or dad might well admit, "I try to build up my children, but what about me? My own parents meant well, but their mistakes undermined my self-esteem, my fourth grade teacher walked all over it, and my junior high basketball coach finished the job. What can I do about feeling inferior and not very gifted? I know God loves me and that Christ died for me, but I have to battle every day to believe I have much real value, compared to so many others I know who are so talented."

All of us have met someone like Gary. He was an only child and his father died when he was three. Gary's mother reared him the only way she knew how—with an iron hand. Believing she needed to establish control while Gary was very young, she used strict guidelines, from which she never deviated under any circumstances. One of her best tools for controlling Gary was remaining aloof and undemonstrative. Gary's mother was sure that any overt displays of affection—lots of kissing, hugging—would damage her image as a disciplinarian.

So little Gary spent his early years trying to win his mother's love and approval. Deep down she did love him dearly, and was very proud of his accomplishments, but Gary never knew it.

Shy, introverted, unsure of himself, Gary went through his teens believing he was a failure, doubting that anyone could ever truly love him, because he was so unlovable. At seventeen he gladly accepted Christ as his Savior at a Young Life meeting, and, while he believed God loved him, he secretly doubted that anyone else could. His mother's parenting style had convinced him he just wasn't worth much. Sure, Christ had died for him, but, after all, Christ died for everyone, losers included. Could other people be that loving? Fat chance.

As he moved into adulthood, Gary strove to overcome his childhood conditioning by working hard—extra hard, as a matter of fact. Slowly but steadily he moved up the ladder at his company, where he was known as "a plodder and not too creative."

Now Gary faces what for him is a tough decision: he's been offered a top job in middle-management that means a substantial increase in pay, perks he's never enjoyed before, and two weeks more vacation each year. But it also means more responsibility and having to oversee several additional people.

"I don't think I'm ready for this," Gary tells his wife. "The job's too big for someone like me. The boss said some nice things at lunch, but if he knew how scared I can get, he would never have made the offer."

Gary's low self-image has given him what could be called a "grasshopper complex." Although that decision for Christ as a teenager stuck and today Gary is an active member of his church and teaching a class of sixth grade boys, he still has the same problems that you can find affecting a lot of people in the Bible. Strangely enough, these people knew God and had actually seen what He could do.

For example, after God brought the children of Israel out of Egypt with enough fireworks to convince even Pharaoh that he was out of his league, they wandered for forty years before coming to Kadesh-Barnea, the gateway to the Promised Land. Moses sent twelve men to check things out, and when they returned the key word on their scouting report was "BIG." The Canaanite warriors were so huge that it made the spies feel like grasshoppers in comparison (see Num. 13:32).

There followed a great uproar. Despite their experience of God's love and care and His awesome demonstrations of power in their lives, the Israelites chickened out. They let a sense of inferiority overwhelm them and it cost them forty more years of wandering in the wilderness before they ever reached the Promised Land. An entire unbelieving generation had to die off before God would let the new generation of Israelites go in.

What does this familiar Old Testament story have to do with someone like Gary and a low self-image? Just like the Israelites, Gary has a "grasshopper complex." His inferior feelings began in his childhood with a mother who thought the best way to rear her boy was with harsh discipline and very little love. Because he thought he could never win his mother's love, Gary wound up feeling unsure of himself, even when he became a rather "successful" adult and was considered in line for a top position in his company.

One of the key signs of feelings of inferiority is that a person will not consider or accept all of the facts. In fact, the person with a low self-image will often look for loopholes in order to find an escape hatch to get out of what he perceives as a difficult situation. The student who has a hard time getting good grades on tests, even though he knows the material, will say, "I guess I'm just not that smart. All I can ever hope for is Cs."

Apparently, only three men among the thousands who stood poised at Kadesh-Barnea ready to take the Promised Land believed it could be done: Caleb, Joshua and Moses. But Moses' faith and leadership weren't enough to turn the tide. The people rebelled and had to pay a terrible price.

If only the Israelites could have listened to Moses, who had learned plenty about trusting God and letting Him handle an inferiority complex. Forty years before he had been wandering around in another desert, caring for his father-in-law's sheep, when God told him he had to go back to Egypt and tell Pharaoh, "Let my people go."

Moses was aghast. Who would listen to him—one man in the face of thousands of armed troops? And, besides, he couldn't even talk well. Somebody with a stutter would be laughed out of Pharaoh's chambers and straight to making bricks without straw with the rest of the Israelite slaves.

But God had an answer for Moses, and it is the starting point for anyone whose self-concept keeps him or her feeling inferior, unworthy and inadequate:

"I will be with you."

We all have Promised Lands to reach and giants to conquer in our lives.

That was all. No analysis of Moses' childhood or the bad break that had put him on the run. No explanation for his stutter, just "I will be with you." And it had been enough—at least up to that point.

But Moses couldn't convince the Israelites that day in the camp at Kadesh-Barnea. Yes, they had seen God's mighty hand make Pharaoh let them go; they had seen God drown Pharaoh's legions in the Red Sea when they tried to follow; they had seen God provide food for them daily with manna, lying to be gathered on the ground; they had seen God defeat their enemies in battle time and again. Nonetheless, the task ahead looked too big and too tough, so they faded.

The result was that God could not be with them, not because God didn't want to be, but because they refused to allow Him. They said: "Under these circumstances, God, we just don't think You can handle it." And God replied, "In that case, I won't. You will die in this desert because you wouldn't believe me."

It's easy enough to see that Gary has come to his own

Kadesh-Barnea, and he has been given an opportunity to go in and take the Promised Land. But the "giants" are waiting and he's afraid. All of us are Garys in one way or another. We all have Promised Lands to reach and giants to conquer in our lives.

Many of us have all kinds of excuses for why we can't do it. "If only you knew what my mother or father was really like. If only you knew what it is like to be black, or crippled, or unattractive, or not as sharp as a lot of the others," and so on and so on.

There are no simplistic answers to conquering feelings of inferiority and low self-image. There is no easy cure for feelings of worthlessness that came from growing up believing that what you did and said weren't important. But the bonds of fear can be broken and it all starts with remembering what God told Moses: "I will be with you."

Some of us might be tempted to mutter under our breath, "No offense, Lord, but I have so many problems and hangups. The sea of life is so wide and my boat is so small."

And God will smile and reply, "Yes, I know, but remember—I've put a lot of work into you. I made you just a little lower than the angels themselves and I've already crowned you with glory and honor. Do you really believe I would let you sink?"

Lord, You know the giants that are in my life and what I need to do. Give me the faith to take that first step.

What are some giants that you face in your own life? How do these giants hold you back or cripple you in some way? What steps of faith (risks) could you take to defeat these giants? How helpful is it to have God say, "I will be with you"?

Notes

1. Ashleigh Brilliant, *I May Not Be Totally Perfect, But Parts of Me Are Excellent* (Santa Barbara: Woodbridge Press Publishing Company, 1979), p. 152.
2. John Lennon and Paul McCartney, "Nowhere Man," (Northern Songs, Ltd./Maclen Music, Inc., 1965).
3. Dorothy Corkille Briggs, *Your Child's Self-Esteem* (New York: Doubleday & Company, Inc., 1970, Dolphin Books Edition, 1975), p. 3.
4. James Dobson, *Hide or Seek* (Old Tappan: Fleming H. Revell Company, 1974), p. 20.

CHAPTER FIFTEEN

If That's All There Is, Will It Be Enough?

"You don't know quite what it is you do want, but it just fairly makes your heart ache you want it so."

—Mark Twain[1]

"All man's efforts are for his mouth, yet his appetite is never satisfied."

—Ecclesiastes 6:7

While I was writing this chapter, we had several couples over for dinner and I decided to do a little informal research. Between bites of salad I asked, "Would you rather be happy or successful?" Responses came thick and fast:

"Let's define 'successful.'"

"Yes, and while we're at it, what does 'happy' mean?"

"If I were happy, that would make me successful."

"Being successful—that sounds like having plenty of money and that doesn't always make you happy, but it certainly helps."

"I think I'd like to be both."

Because so many of our friends' answers centered around definitions, I went to my trusty *American Heritage* dictionary for some help. It tells me that "happy" means "characterized by luck or good fortune; prosperous."[2]

As for defining "successful," that same dictionary says, "Having obtained something desired or intended; having achieved wealth or eminence."[3]

One problem with hoping to be happy is that the word comes from the root word *hap*, which means chance or luck. Our Declaration of Independence guarantees us the right to life, liberty and the pursuit of happiness, but it does not guarantee that we will always find it. You can pursue happiness through materialism, pleasure-seeking, power-grabs, or just plain hard work, but there are no guarantees. What you learn is that you really can't pursue happiness, because happiness is a by-product of a certain approach to living.

As for success, there are all kinds of ways to pursue that, too: making a lot of money, acquiring fame or power, or achieving a false kind of "self-fulfillment," based on satisfying your appetites and gaining your share of creature comforts.

Writing in *Waking from the American Dream,* Donald McCullough defines "fulfilled" as an unambiguous peace, a sense that you've become all you were meant to be. But have you ever met anyone who feels *totally* fulfilled? I haven't either. No matter how far along the path to maturity the Lord may bring us, we all feel a certain sense of unfinished business. Only the Lord Jesus Himself could die saying, "It is finished," and mean exactly that. As McCullough writes: "What's normal is living with a sense of incompleteness, the feeling that we have unfinished business at the center of our lives."[4]

Perhaps no group in our present society knows better the feelings of unfulfillment than the Yuppies who dominated much of the thinking and writing about success in the 1980s. But according to the *Boomer Report,* a marketing newsletter aimed at the baby boomer generation, the Yuppies have become the MOSS generation, meaning "Middle-aged, Overstressed, Semi-affluent, Suburbanites."

According to those who have coined this new acronym, the typical MOSS is forty-one, working on a second marriage, has 2.0 biological and .5 stepchildren, owns at least one publication on cholesterol, and is affluent, but doesn't feel that way.[5]

During the 1980s, leading periodicals across the country would frequently carry stories of men and women who would reach the pinnacle of financial and corporate success, suffer burnout and decide to pack it in and get out while they still had their sanity. One such case was Susan Wolfson, who arrived in New York in her early twenties with a B.A. in history and no particular goal except to be part of the metropolis she felt was the hub of the world.[6] That was 1975, and by 1977 she had acquired a job at *Family Circle* magazine as a production assistant. By 1981 she had married Joe Kovach, who was then the news editor of the *New York Daily News*. Not long after, she was contacted by Rowlands, one of the top PR firms in Manhattan, and took a job that put her on a fast track straight to the top.

When Susan arrived at her new job, at a substantial increase in salary and with her own office facing Madison Avenue, she could see nothing but success and more success ahead. The first thing she noticed was that everyone seemed to be running everywhere, talking faster and moving faster. With savvy and tenacity, she plunged into her work, which included accounts like *Esquire and Cosmopolitan*. Susan moved quickly up the ladder and that Christmas a senior vice president rewarded her with a silver business card holder, engraved with her initials. It made her feel as if she had "really arrived."

In her second year at Rowlands, she became absolutely immersed in her work, which was more than just a job, it was her "career." With no time to go out to lunch with friends, she had take-out delivered to her office and kept working right through lunch. She had picked up the signals that told her, "If you have a peaceful day around here, you are a loser."

That summer and into the fall, she lost one account but gained others, and by December she was so busy there was no time for Christmas shopping. In her words, "Work annihilated Christmas...everything that used to be a pleasure became a chore."

During the next year, Susan joined a women's health club a few blocks from her office, and became the consummate professional, wearing the latest in expensive styles and thriving on deadlines. High gear wasn't fast enough for her. Stress was like an aphrodisiac.

Susan's incredible pace, plus her husband's own busy schedule, didn't do much for their relationship. They would plan to get away on weekends, but end up having to cancel because one or the other would have to work. A special dinner out in celebration of her thirtieth birthday turned into bickering and they went home without even ordering.

A few months later, their wedding anniversary didn't fare much better. Despite a new $140 "life organizer," which was supposed to enable her to "do it all," Susan continued to run out of energy and motivation. While she was visiting relatives, someone asked her what her next step was, and she replied, "Vice president." Would that make her happy? someone wanted to know. Susan's answer: "No."

On the plane back to New York, she took stock of her "success." She traveled with name brand luggage, shopped at name brand department stores, and ate at the finest restaurants. Every five weeks she had another $70 hairstyle. She dressed in the finest clothes and used a bundle of credit cards to run up monthly bills of more than $1500. Currently, she was shopping for a Rolex watch and a country house.

Then it struck her. She had been totally sucked into the "success trap." She realized that no matter how hard she worked, life wouldn't become any more fulfilling (if it had ever been fulfilling at all). She wasn't the kind of friend she wanted to be, or the kind of wife she wanted to be. She started realizing that having it all was like a dog chasing its tail and that she always ended up with "having very little."

Something had to give, and it did. In less than two months, she sat down with two executive vice-presidents who were her immediate superiors and told them, "I've decided to leave the Rowland company." Reluctantly, they accepted her resignation and, at the age of thirty,

Susan Wolfson was off the fast track, wondering how she would adapt to a stress-free life.

The only thing she kept from her former life was her morning aerobics class at the health club, and she settled into what she felt was slow motion living, getting to know her husband, doing volunteer work and perfecting kitchen skills that she never had time for before. As the months went by, she finally did take on some free-lance assignments for spending money, but she vowed she would never again allow work to "become the main event" in her life.

Susan Wolfson's story sounds like what Oscar Wilde said about the two greatest tragedies in life: not getting what you want, and then getting it.

No one would understand Oscar Wilde's quip better than King Solomon who started out as "the wisest man who ever lived." He also became one of the most success-ful, if you define success as making it big time with the bucks, the homes and palaces, the chariots, the clothes, the sumptuous banquets and women galore. But despite all his success, Solomon died an unhappy failure. In fact, he lived a lot of his life unhappily, trying to figure out his kids, not to mention some seven hundred wives and three hundred concubines.

Near the end of his days, Solomon came to the same conclusion Susan Wolfson did on that plane: that life was not very fulfilling (see Eccles. 1:2,3).

Although there is some disagreement, many biblical scholars believe that Ecclesiastes is Solomon's autobio-graphical admission that he tried to find success on his own and it all turned out to be sawdust in his mouth.[7] You name it, Solomon tried to find it in his quest for satis-faction and happiness apart from God: pleasure, laughter, drinking bouts, building his own equivalent of the Trump

Tower, owning huge herds of animals, as well as harems and many slaves. This king refused his heart no pleasure (see Eccles. 2:10).

As Solomon lists what hasn't worked, he also drops hints about what always does. For example, in Ecclesiastes 2:26 he says, "To the man who pleases him, God gives wis-

---

Success is in the eyes of the beholder, and, for the follower of Christ, success means beholding God first and then doing what pleases Him.

---

dom, knowledge and happiness, but to the sinner he gives the task of gathering and storing up wealth to hand it over to the one who pleases God." In Ecclesiastes 8:12, he speaks of wicked men who might commit one hundred crimes and still live long lives, but he knows "it will go better with God-fearing men, who are reverent before God."

But in chapter 12, Solomon shows his real hand. The first eleven chapters have been his confession, the twelfth chapter is his word to the wise. To the young he says, "Remember your Creator in the days of your youth, before the days of trouble come" (Eccles. 12:1).

And in his final line, the preacher gives this advice: "Fear God and keep his commandments, for this is the whole duty of man. For God will bring every deed into judgment, including every hidden thing, whether it is good or evil" (Eccles. 12:13,14).

Solomon had it all, but it hadn't been enough. What is enough? Faithful obedience to God. That is what true success is all about. To steal a line from Gordon Gekko, the corporate pirate of the film, *Wall Street,* "All the rest is conversation."

In Hebrews 11, God's "Hall of Fame of Faith" includes mighty leaders like Moses, rich men like Abraham, and rulers of kingdoms like Joseph. But as the list continues, we read of others who go unnamed, but who are tortured, flogged, chained and imprisoned for their faith, yet remain true. Some are stoned, others are sawed in half or impaled on a sword. Some go about in sheepskins and goatskins, destitute, persecuted and mistreated. They wander through deserts and mountains, living in caves and holes in the ground. Somehow these unfortunate souls are seldom mentioned by preachers of the Gospel of Prosperity or the numerous hawkers of success in real estate who assure you that you will "make a lot of money" if you attend their seminar or buy their sets of tapes, which have just been marked down to $179.95.

Truly, success is in the eyes of the beholder, and, for the follower of Christ, success means beholding God first and then doing what pleases Him. The writers of the Westminster catechism knew all about success. That's why they opened with: "Man's chief end is to glorify God and to enjoy Him forever." It's possible for the Christian also to enjoy riches, fame and whatever God chooses to send his way. But all that is secondary to what is primary.

In the spring of 1989, seventeen-year-old Michael Chang stunned the tennis world by becoming the youngest player ever to win the French Open. His endorsements alone exceed one million dollars annually. He looks forward to career winnings that will run into many millions more. But Chang, who makes his faith in

Christ plain in television interviews, realizes that all this money and fame is not what his life is all about.

One day as he was talking to the media, he grappled with the whole question of luck, fortune or what people call "fate." He mentioned that he often thought about why there is life on this planet. There must be a reason, otherwise we would all live and die and our lives would mean nothing. As for becoming the best tennis player in the world, Chang leaves that in God's hands. He is ready for defeat as well as victory, and he says, "I think there will be times that maybe I won't be doing so well and I'm sure people will be saying, 'So where is your Jesus Christ?'

"For me", said Chang, "I feel as if being a Christian I have a job to do on this earth, and that's my first priority—to get that job done. You can't win all the time. You can only do as much as you are made to do."[8]

---

*Lord, help me do what You made me to do,
no more, no less.*

Write your personal definition of success. On a scale of 1 to 10 (ten meaning making excellent progress), how are you doing at living a successful life? If your score is lower than you would like, how do you need to change?

Notes
1. Public domain.
2. William Morris, Editor, *The American Heritage Dictionary of the English Language* (New York and Boston: American Heritage Publishing Company, Inc., and Houghton Mifflin Company, 1969), p. 599.
3. The *American Heritage Dictionary of the English Language*, p. 1285.

4. Donald W. McCullough, *Waking from the American Dream* (Downers Grove: InterVarsity Press, 1988), p. 60.
5. "The MOSS Generation," *Effective Ministries Update,* Vol. 1, Number 12, August, 1989, p. 1.
6. See Dinah Prince, "Why One Wonder Woman Packed It In," *New York,* July 15, 1985, pp. 42-47.
7. Henrietta Mears, *What the Bible Is All About* (Ventura: Regal Books, 1953), p. 201.
8. See Thomas Bonk, "Boy Wonder," *Los Angeles Times,* August 27, 1989, pp. 8-16.

CHAPTER SIXTEEN

Workaholism Is a Real Disease

"The workaholic...enjoys nothing except an occasional good meal, constant supplies of work, and a good bed to fall into from sheer exhaustion. This goes on until death."

—Wayne Oates,
Confessions of a Workaholic [1]

"In vain you rise early and stay up late, toiling for food to eat—for he grants sleep to those he loves."

—Psalm 127:2

The "pursuit of success," which characterized the past decade, left its own legacy, including some who realized in time that there is more to life than books like *Getting Yours* try to suggest. As we sat at lunch, Hugh shared with me what it had been like back in 1982 when he was thirty something, pursuing success in a middle management sales job for a medium sized publishing firm.

Married, with three small sons aged two and up, Hugh was a baby boomer who believed life was good and it was only a matter of time until he reached the top. Yes, there were pressures, particularly financial, because his salary was modest, but Hugh believed that automatic advancement would eventually take him up the ladder to "success."

Meanwhile, Hugh felt just working was success enough. He loved his job, and when he came to Friday night, he always felt gnawing disappointment, because he realized he'd have to spend the next two days away from his job. Actually, while his body did spend weekends at home, his mind stayed at the office. By Sunday evening he could actually feel the adrenaline starting to pump again as he anticipated Monday morning.

Although he didn't realize it, Hugh was meeting his emotional needs at work, not at home. His wife sensed it in his preoccupation and lack of interest in her and the boys. He wasn't unkind, out of sorts or mean—but mentally he just wasn't there. As Hugh described his daily routine at work, he told me:

> Ironically, I didn't push myself that hard during the day, because I secretly knew I had until 6:00 or 7:00 that night to finish up. I'd spend some time during the day socializing, talking on the phone or wandering down the hall to check something with

someone else. Then, when most people had gone home, I'd crack down and say, "Oh, my gosh, I've got to get a few things done today."

As a rule Hugh would do more work between 4:00 and 7:00 P.M. than he did between 8:00 A.M. and 4:00 P.M. True, a lot of people have jobs where they could blame this kind of routine on the day's interruptions. But for Hugh, interruptions weren't really the problem. As a rule, he could have been a lot more productive during the day and could have left on time to go home, but he was just enjoying his job too much. He recalled:

> I just plain liked talking business and discussing whatever project I was working on at the time. I was having more fun at work than I was going to have at home because I knew when I got there, there were kids who wanted to play with me, and a wife who wanted me to deal with problems and do chores around the house. None of that was anywhere nearly as ego satisfying as being at work.

The more Hugh talked, the more I realized he was exhibiting many of the symptoms of a workaholic (it takes one to know one). "Workaholic" is such a familiar term that many people think it has always been part of our vocabulary, but not so. It is a *neologism*, a semi-humorous word invented by seminary professor Wayne Oates when he wrote *Confessions of a Workaholic* in 1971.

Oates' definition of workaholism is similar to the World Health Organization's definition of alcoholism. According to Oates, a workaholic is "a person whose need for work has become so excessive that it creates a noticeable disturbance or interference with his (or her) bodily health, personal happiness, interpersonal relations, and smooth social functioning."[2]

Hugh didn't fit every part of that definition, but his love for work definitely affected his functioning as a husband and father. While he was never in danger of slipping into an affair with somebody at work (his "socializing" was always at the business level with anyone willing to talk), his marriage was headed for trouble and only a reversal in his climb up the career ladder brought him to his senses.* In truth, Hugh's symptoms of workaholism were rather mild compared to the "dyed in the wool" workaholic described by Oates and other counselors. Some of the classic signs are these:

1. *Workaholics put in a long day.* They often talk about how early they got to work and how late they remained and how little sleep they got the night before. It is not unusual for a Christian workaholic businessman to get to the office by 7:00 A.M. so he can have "quiet time" and then stay until 9:00 or 10:00 P.M. to get all his work done. Commonly, hard core workaholics will maintain a fifteen-hour pace for six days a week.[3]

2. Workaholics love to talk about how much they get done—the size of their reports, the number of calls they made last month, the number of people they handle, and so on and so forth. Rarely do workaholics talk about their families unless they want to mention how hard they're working for them.[4]

3. A telltale sign of most workaholics is their inability to say no to people who just have to see

---

*The rest of Hugh's story is in chapters 25 and 26.

them, or who need their help or services. Workaholics seem to think they have no limitations and they just take on more and more. In truth, what is often limited is their self-esteem. The reason they take on more and more is to please others and be accepted. Along with feeling they have no limits to their energy, workaholics often have a false sense of superiority. They trust only themselves and their work. They secretly assume they are indispensable and openly proclaim, "If I don't do this, who will?"

4. Other signs of workaholism are cardiac or circulatory problems. Dr. Meyer Friedman, co-author of the best-selling book, Type A Behavior and Your Heart, has done numerous studies showing that Americans suffer from clogging of the heart arteries more than any other group on earth. Ironically, this has nothing to do with race, diet, or even smoking. Friedman compared Japanese males with American males and the findings showed that, although the Japanese smoked 50 percent more than their American counterparts, they experienced only 10 percent as much heart disease. Friedman believes that the chief culprit is stress, which is obviously part of the workaholic's tense, driven life-style.[5]

Because we all seem to be under stress, workaholism is a widely accepted social disease. We agonize over and treat the alcoholic, but we give the workaholic a pat on the back and shove him back into the rat race with cheers and shouting. In 1971, Wayne Oates observed, "Excessive work is lauded, praised, expected and often demanded of a person in America." In the 1980s, the greedy drive to be rich and successful made this almost doubly true. According to the Harris Poll, by 1987 the average work week had climbed to 48.6 hours, up from 40.6 in 1973. During that same period, leisure time shrank from 26.2 hours a week down to 16.2.[6]

One corporate consultant who travels the country began noticing a definite upswing in addiction to work by 1982. Most of the people he dealt with felt they could work seven days a week, twenty-four hours a day, and not get done with their work loads.[7]

We agonize over and treat the alcoholic, but we give the workaholic a pat on the back and shove him back into the rat race with cheers and shouting.

But there is a limit to everything, even work addiction, and by the end of the '80s many burned out workaholics were saying they'd had enough. The media began carrying stories about people who were deciding to get out of the rat race and do something less strenuous and less time consuming so they could have more time with their families.

When a workaholic finally bottoms out, he sounds a great deal like another famous workaholic of ancient times—King Solomon. Solomon amazed the world with his capacity for work, but toward the end of his life he admitted:

> So I hated life, because the work that is done under the sun was grievous to me. All of it is meaningless, a chasing after the wind....What does a man

get for all the toil and anxious striving with which
he labors under the sun? All his days his work is
pain and grief; even at night his mind does not rest.
This too is meaningless (Eccles. 2:17,22,23).

I mentioned that Hugh's workaholic symptoms were
easy to spot because "it takes one to know one." At times
over the years, I have been able to identify quite well with
Solomon, especially with that part about the mind not
resting very well at night. Working in Christian writing
and publishing is a great way to get your mind going non-
stop and, as a perfectionist who loved to perform and
achieve, workaholic tendencies were part of my makeup.

I tried to get one hundred percent results every time,
and I was merciless in making demands upon myself and
others. I was intolerant of incompetence, over-committed
my employers, and prone to take on more and more
assignments to please more and more people. As Wayne
Oates describes the workaholic:

He is likely to take on more and more over and
above the prescribed activities, thus he collides
with himself in the face of the many demands laid
upon him: he is a perfectionist, but he commits
himself to so many people for the use of his skills
that he cannot do his job well. This results in an
anxiety depression amounting to panic. His sleep is
more and more curtailed by the sheer problems of
scheduling and by his effort to prepare for his
responsibilities when he should be sleeping. The
morass of contradictory demands is too deep for
him to extricate himself, and something has to be
done by others to rescue him. His life has become
unmanageable.[8]

Many of the symptoms Oates described were mine, especially when I was on another deadline push. Fortunately, working with Sunday School curriculum constantly exposes you to Scripture, and the Lord was able to talk to me even while I indulged in my workaholism. He was able to get through to me just as he got through to Solomon, who realized: "A man can do nothing better than to eat and drink and find satisfaction in his work. This too, I see, is from the hand of God, *for without him*, who can eat or find enjoyment?" (Eccles. 2:24,25, italics mine).

It's easy to read a book like Ecclesiastes and think it's only the pessimistic prattle of an old man who backslid from his faith and got burned out on life. But every now and then we can find Solomon remembering his roots and pointing to the answer to all of this "meaninglessness." I agree with Frank Wichern, a clinical psychologist who believes the book of Ecclesiastes dramatizes the need for a dynamic relationship with a living, loving God. Wichern writes:

> When we know God, we have new alternatives, new ways of understanding life. We have new ways of relating to life. The performance standard is out. Being able to enjoy what is being done now is in. The alternative of Ecclesiastes 2:24 is that in God's plan there are simple pleasures in life, and these pleasures are a by-product of one's relationship to God.[9]

Ironically, I slipped toward workaholism after becoming well acquainted with God and being fully aware of the new alternatives He had given me for life. I got so wrapped up in "my ministry" I forgot life's simple pleasures. I got so busy serving God I forgot how to enjoy Him, even though

I thought I was glorifying Him. How I turned the corner is the subject of the next chapter.

Lord, may I never forget that without You
there is no pleasure in life.

Go back over this chapter and check to see if you have any symptoms of workaholism. Do you work long hours? Do you tend to talk about how much work you do? Do you talk about your work more than your family? Do you find it hard to say no to additional assignments? Is your blood pressure where it should be?

Notes

1. Wayne Oates, *Confessions of a Workaholic* (New York: The World Publishing Company, 1971), p. 10. Oates is paraphrasing an observation made by William H. Whyte, *The Organization Man* (New York: Touchstone Books, 1972).
2. Ibid., p. 4.
3. See Frank B. Wichern, "'All Is Vanity,' Saith the Exhausted Executive," *Eternity*, November 1982, p. 23. Also see Wayne Oates, *Confessions of a Workaholic*, p. 7.
4. See Frank B. Wichern, *Eternity*, November 1981, p. 3.
5. See Melvin D. Schmidt, "Schedaholism," *The Mennonite*, June 26, 1979.
6. See Joan Libman, "Why We Overwork," *Los Angeles Times*, Monday, June 13, 1988, Part V, p. 1.
7. Joan Libman, "Why We Overwork," Part V, p. 1.
8. Wayne Oates, *Confessions of a Workaholic*, pp. 60,61.
9. Frank B. Wichern, "'All Is Vanity' Saith the Exhausted Executive," Eternity, November 1981, p. 24.

CHAPTER SEVENTEEN

Workaholic?
Try Ten Days of Rest and Regular Weekend Follow-ups

"It is dangerous for a Christian to live on his physical capital. We have no more right to overwork than to under-work. It is wiser to *burn on than to burn out.*"

—W. Graham Scroggie[1]

"My son, if you accept my words and store up my commands within you,...then you will understand the fear of the Lord and find the knowledge of God."

—Proverbs 2:1,5

If you're like me, you're not sure you want to admit to being a "hard core" or "dyed in the wool" workaholic. Ed Dayton, director of World Vision's Advance Research and Communications Center, defines workaholism as being addicted to work. He writes:

> We understand the idea of a drug addict, tobacco addict or alcoholic, but don't think often of the "workaholic." Possibly one of the most unique and destructive of all addictions is the *compulsion* to work...what adds to the seriousness of the problem is that it often goes untreated because it is the only addiction that often makes one look like a saint.[2]

Dayton believes that "the well-adjusted personality can work with joy and deep satisfaction, but for the workaholic, the job becomes his god and the place of work is the shrine." If you suspect you may be a workaholic, try answering these questions:

1. Do you find it difficult to become involved in activities other than your job?
2. Does "doing nothing" drive you up the wall?
3. How do you view hobbies or sports? Are they a "should" or a "must" instead of a "want to"?[3]

Keep in mind, of course, that there is a difference between someone who loves his or her work and a work addict. As Wayne Oates puts it, "There is nothing inherently wrong with work. Everybody sooner or later gets around to it, even if only in the form of exertion to avoid work!"[4]

The work lover may put in long hours, but it isn't wearing because it's enjoyable. Mark Twain was a work lover and, as he neared the end of his productive life, he observed that he "hadn't done a lick of work in over fifty years." He said, "I've always been able to gain my living without doing any work; for the writing of books and magazine matter was always play, not work. I enjoyed it; it was merely billiards to me."[5]

A key difference between the workaholic and the lover of work is that the one who loves his work can stop any time he wants to, but the work addict can't. He'll use excuses such as the staff being cut down and having to double up his hours in order to get the same work load out. But deep down, there are other reasons.

Some workaholics slave long hours to get the approval of others; other workaholics put in those long hours to get approval of themselves, which is often true of perfectionists who bite off more than they can chew (see chapter 18). For years this was my problem and I still battle the same tendency, but now, at least, I am aware of what I'm doing to myself and those close to me.

Fortunately, there are ways to break the shackles of workaholism or what you might detect as the beginnings of work addiction.

Step One is to admit the problem. It might even help to go look in the mirror and say, "I am a workaholic, or at least I'm in danger of becoming one."

This may be especially hard for you if you are earning your living in some phase of Christian ministry or if a lot of your workaholism comes out through your over involvement in your church. In my case, it came out in both ways: not only was I overinvolved at work in a Christian publishing house, but I was so committed at church I had no spare time left for much of anything else. I can recall going to one year-end banquet at my church and getting up six or seven times to acknowledge the "recognition" for being chairman of this or a key member of that committee.

As Ed Dayton observes, Christians may be trying to prove they are really in God's business by how hard they work. They can begin to change by understanding that God will get His work done at His pace, not the workaholic's.[6] As much as Jesus accomplished in three short years of earthly ministry, no one would ever picture Him as a workaholic.

Jesus moved about quietly and effectively, teaching, preaching, and healing, never falling victim to what one writer has called "schedaholism," an irrational addiction to schedules, wanting everything to run exactly on time, and being irritated if there might be a few minutes, or even a few seconds, to wait.

Melvin Schmidt, who now has a pastorate in Ohio, spent four years in Southeast Asia as a missionary and had to learn to adjust to what was called "rubber" time. In the Asian culture, if a meeting were scheduled for 7:30 p.m., people often didn't show up until 8:30. Schmidt's Indonesian friends were content with operating according to rubber time, but he was not. Schmidt spent many frustrated hours wondering if a meeting would ever start so he could get back home and get "on schedule again." He writes:

> One of my Asian friends once told me that the most ridiculous situation imaginable is an American missionary who has ulcers telling a Hindu sage all about "peace of mind." I discovered that ulcers are almost unknown in Southeast Asia, neither is high blood pressure, neither is the typical heart attack as we know it.[7]

Granted, "rubber time" wouldn't work very well in our

culture. Showing up late is viewed as inconsiderate—or worse. But as we all synchronize our chronographs, complete with stopwatch mode, we might pause to ask ourselves if we are so addicted to schedules and work loads that we have forgotten to do what a "pagan" Asian culture understands intuitively—how to rest and relax.

What hard core or even fringe workaholics need to come to grips with is that work is their idol, not just their mission or ministry.

Before we go any further, it is worth noting that workaholism is hardly an exclusively male problem. With almost 60 percent of all wives and mothers currently involved in the work force, plenty of women are learning about the addictions of workaholism. In fact, as a woman rises within an organization, she may get sucked into the work trap because of the adrenaline high she can get from being on the inside and having power unknown to her in the past. Even homemakers are not immune, particularly the perfectionists who want everything just right, and whose schedule would cause the busiest CEO to gasp in dismay.

Step Two in breaking work addiction is to plan your rest. This may sound a little crazy, but if you plan your rest you may actually stop and let it happen! Actually, it shouldn't be all that difficult. All we need to do is follow the master plan laid down by the Lord Himself in Genesis, chapter one: six days on and one day off.

God's example of resting after six days of creative work is only the beginning in an Old Testament pattern of rest and worship that not only included a Sabbath every week, but a Sabbath year every seven years, which meant that the land was not to be sown or reaped, the vineyards pruned, or the fruits gathered in. Spontaneous growth of field and orchard was free to all, debtors were released from their obligations and any Israelites in bondage to their countrymen were given their freedom.

Unfortunately, the letter of the law overcame the spirit of the law and, by the time of Christ's earthly ministry, the Pharisees had turned the Sabbath into an incredible list of nit-picking rules that made hard work out of not working. Many of Jesus' disagreements with the Pharisees were over His healing someone on the Sabbath, which they considered work and, therefore, breaking the Law.

The Pharisees missed the real point of the Sabbath, but we have taken the freedom we have in Christ and have pushed it too far. We are also missing the point by failing to stop and rest, and excusing it by saying, "We're not legalistic. After all, the Sabbath was made for man, and not man for the Sabbath!"

Step Three involves anticipating the benefits of rest. Workaholics, in particular, seem to dread Sundays and claim they can't get much rest at all because they are still thinking about that work load back at the office. Some of them even sneak back to the office on Sunday, or haul it home and work on it anyway.

What hard-core or even fringe workaholics need to come to grips with is that work is their idol, not just their mission or ministry. A good question for any workaholic to ask himself or herself is, "Who am I really trying to please?" As Ed Dayton observes, "We need to remember that our rest and worship pleases God. *There is more to life than work. Rest is as pleasing to God as work*" (italics mine).[8]

It has taken me many years to begin to understand the

true significance of applying the above three steps to my life. I can remember my first decision to try to change, which I made during a Christmas Eve service in my church. I don't remember what was preached or sung, but I do remember asking God to help me spend more time with my family—and, more important, with Him. It has been slow going. I was so hooked on work that one of my favorite poems was Rudyard Kipling's intriguing picture of heaven:

> When Earth's last picture is painted, and the tubes
>   are twisted and dried,
> When the oldest colours have faded, and the youngest
>   critic has died,
> We shall rest, and, faith, we shall need it—
>   lie down for an aeon or two,
> Till the Master of all good workmen
>   shall put us to work anew.[9]

I still like the imagery in Kipling's poem, but his theology falls a bit short. No part of eternity is to be spent in work. Scripture teaches that we are to rest (see Heb. 4; Rev. 14:13). As for activities, our major pastime will be praising God (see Rev. 7:9-17) alongside those we have brought into the Kingdom, especially loved ones. In the late '60s, several years before Wayne Oates coined the term "workaholic," Ray Stevens wrote "Mr. Businessman," a catchy tune that climbed to the top of the charts. The probing lyrics suggest several good questions for anyone spending too much time "taking care of business":[10]

> Am I taking time to really see my children grow up?
> Those roses in the garden—have I ever really smelled them?

Does the morning sun warm my soul and brighten my day, or is it simply a signal to punch the clock again?

Am I truly living or am I just surviving?

Whenever the tentacles of workaholism seem to wrap themselves around my busy schedule, I try to stop and remember questions like these. No matter how busy things get, we always have a choice: we can live life more abundantly or we can work continuously—and simply survive.

Lord, don't let work loads disqualify me from really living. Remind me every day that there is more to life than work.

In addition to the three steps outlined in this chapter, also try the following to rid yourself of workaholism:

1. Take fearless inventory of all the busy-work you do and then throw it overboard. Take on no additional work assignments until you can "sleep on/pray about it" and talk it over with your spouse or another trusted person.
2. Spend time each weekend in meditation, alone with God, thinking about what really matters and does not matter in your life. Get rid of what doesn't matter.
3. Remember what you used to enjoy doing while growing up or when you were first married. Try to revive some of those practices for recreation and fun.
4. If you like reading, choose relaxing reading that

you don't have to do at work. It doesn't have to be "a classic" or on the best-seller list. Or, pick some TV shows that are relaxing and watch them without apology. There are ways to use the boob tube as therapy.

5. Try renewing contacts with people with whom you've "lost touch." Try dropping them a brief line, a phone call or possibly getting together for lunch.[11]

Notes

1. W. Graham Scroggie, *The Gospel of Mark* (Grand Rapids: Zondervan Publishing House, 1979), p. 119.
2. Ed Dayton, "The Work Trap" *Christian Leadership Letter,* Ministry of World Vision International, November 1979, p. 1.
3. Ibid., p. 1.
4. Wayne Oates, *Confessions of a Workaholic,* (New York: World Publishing Company, 1971), p. 6.
5. Quoted by Ed Dayton in "The Work Trap," p. 2, original source unknown.
6. See Edward R. Dayton, "Harried and Hurried," *Christian Leadership Letter,* April-May, 1989, World Vision, p. 15.
7. Melvin D. Schmidt, "Schedaholism," *The Mennonite,* June 26, 1979.
8. Edward R. Dayton, *Christian Leadership Letter,* p. 15.
9. From "L'Envoi," quoted in *English Literature, A Period Anthology,* edited by Albert C. Baugh and George William McClelland (New York: Appleton-Century-Crofts, Inc., 1954), p. 1412.
10. See Ray Stevens, "Mr. Businessman," (Monument Records, July 1968).
11. Adapted from Wayne Oates, *Confessions of a Workaholic,* pp. 30, 31.

CHAPTER EIGHTEEN

Those Who Raise Bar Too High Fall Flat on Face

"Perfectionism is slow suicide."
—Dr. Kevin Leman

"My grace is sufficient for you, for my power is made perfect in your imperfections."
—2 Corinthians 12:9 (paraphrased)

"I should have *gotten it done sooner*, but..."

"Well, I guess it's okay, but I could do better *if I had more time.*"

"If it's worth doing, it's worth taking the time to do it right!"

"Why, yes, I think I have time to help with that."

Any of these sound familiar? Perhaps you have said something similar recently (for example, in the last thirty minutes). If so, it could mean:

1. You're pretty normal—caught in the time crunch like millions of others and coping as best as you can.
2. You're an efficiency nut—always organized, not wasting a second, the envy of everyone on your block or at your work place (members of your family probably aren't so envious because you are probably driving them bonkers).
3. You're a perfectionist—the type who is most susceptible to getting sucked into the rat race because you're always biting off more than you can chew.

This chapter and the next are for perfectionists, written by a perfectionist who suspects he has a lot of company. In *Healing for Damaged Emotions*, Dr. David Seamands confirms my suspicions: "Perfectionism is the most disturbing emotional problem among evangelical Christians. It walks into my office more often than any other single Christian hangup."[1]

My wife, Jackie, once defined perfectionism as "trying to be perfect beyond reason," the shortest and best explanation I've ever heard. Perfectionism is not the pursuit of excellence, which is an attempt to meet high standards within your reach. Perfectionists, however, tend to dance to an "all or nothing" tune that demands inappropriately high standards.

Instead of trying to do their best, perfectionists try to be the best.

Instead of saying, "I will," perfectionists say, "I should," or "I ought."

Instead of being motivated by a desire for success, perfectionists are driven by a fear of failure.

In short, perfectionists are especially vulnerable to becoming too busy, frantically rushing about saying, "If only I had more time—then I could do a really good job!"

I've often used that last excuse myself—after dashing to the deadline on another book project. In fact, I've been informally diagnosed as a perfectionist by Dr. Kevin Leman, a psychologist with whom I've worked as an acquisitions editor for major publishing firms. He nailed me one night while we were having dinner together after a hard day chewing on his latest manuscript.

"Perfectionism," said Dr. Leman, "is slow suicide, and you may be a candidate."

"How so?"

"Because you are an only child—a discouraged perfectionist."

"Who, me?" I said with a short laugh. "I always thought I was the one who discouraged perfectionists, like my wife who has been trying to teach me to hang up my clothes for over thirty years. Besides, my yard looks like Safari Land, U.S.A., and I haven't seen the top of my desk in eight years."

"Messiness is quite typical in discouraged perfectionists," Dr. Leman replied. "When you were very young, you learned that you can't always be perfect, so you work that out by being messy, while still trying to reach the standards you've set. I watch you while we work on my manuscripts, you are a real flaw-picker."

"Well, I admit I'm fussy—that's my job—but I'm still

not convinced that I'm a perfectionist. I often don't reach all my goals or standards."

"Exactly. I'll bet you start a lot of projects and never finish them, don't you?"

"Well...that's true, I guess. It's just that I have so many things to get done. I have to let some of them go."

"That's typical of a perfectionist, the Big Picture gets him down. He often winds up procrastinating or just muddling along."

"I do have trouble getting started sometimes with a writing or editing job, but I always go to the whip in the stretch and usually make the deadlines."

"More typical perfectionist behavior. You need a deadline to force you to produce. It's part of your total self-image. You gain a lot of your self-esteem at being good at what you do. That's often caused by a critical parent. Were one of your parents overly critical?"

"Well, as a matter of fact, my dad was always on my case, as well as Mom's."

"That's part of the reason why you think of the negative side first—editors are born critics. They can't help it or they wouldn't be editors."

"And all this means I'm committing slow suicide?"

"Well, that's a typical Leman exaggeration, but perfectionists do put a lot of stress on themselves. You're the all-or-nothing type, always pushing to get it 'exactly right.' Perfectionism is your strength, but it's also your weakness."

Following that conversation with Kevin, I did some heavy thinking and decided that he had me pegged pretty well. Not long afterward, everything he said was confirmed when I read a book by another psychologist friend, Dr. David Stoop (*Living with a Perfectionist*).[2]

From Dave's book I learned that perfectionists are "dichotomous thinkers"—that is, they see everything as either-or or all-or-nothing. Of course, this kind of thinking traps perfectionists into believing that everything they do must be thorough and superbly exceptional. Anything else is a failure, or at least something that causes self-criticism. Perfectionists have a hard time saying, "Well, it was good

---

Instead of being motivated by a desire for success, perfectionists are driven by a fear of failure.

---

enough." Usually, it's not good enough, and that's where the self-criticism comes in.

Right along with all this is the perfectionist's habit of setting too many goals that are too far out of reach. Goal setting is a wonderful tool (as we'll see in chapter 22), but when you set unrealistic goals, trying to get too much done too fast, it leads to frustration or at best, partial success.

It's no wonder that perfectionists get overwhelmed by what Kevin called "The Big Picture." It's also called "the hurdle effect," which happens when the perfectionist sets all those impossible goals and then looks into the immediate future—everything he has to do that day, for example—and realizes that he'll just never make it. There is just too much to do!

Feeling overwhelmed doesn't help the perfectionist's negative outlook on life. The old cliché calls it "seeing the glass half empty." It's also called "maximizing and minimizing" (or the "M&M" principle)—maximizing your failures and minimizing your successes. Perfectionists do this in hundreds of ways. For example, the perfectionist homemaker (who may have spent the day wearing her other hat at the office) puts together a sensational meal and her dinner guests tell her it was "absolutely perfect."

"Well, it wasn't too bad," she replies, "but I do think the plum sauce for the chicken had a bit too much mustard, myself."

And if you want to reverse the picture, you can easily see how this same lady could maximize her failures. If something did go wrong with her dinner, it wouldn't be a matter of saying, "So the meat wasn't tender, everything else was good." Instead, the whole dinner would be a "total disaster."

The terrible price perfectionists pay when they let the M&M principle run wild is that they don't simply evaluate a performance and learn from the mistakes. Instead, they internalize all their errors and dwell on them. The seeker of excellence rates his or her performance and moves on, but perfectionists rate themselves. Everything they do becomes a barometer of personal worth.

This is why perfectionists almost always have "The Avis Complex." They're always trying harder. Nothing is ever good enough, even if people tell them it's outstanding. At the end of the chapter is a diagram and brief explanation of the endless cycles of frustration and exhaustion caused by perfectionism.[3] It's easy enough to see why Christians are often sucked into this pursuit of being perfect. After all, isn't that what God wants? Didn't Jesus Himself say, "You are to be perfect, like your Heavenly Father"?[4]

And what about the lament of Paul the Apostle, who certainly must qualify as a candidate for "outstanding perfectionist of all time." In Romans 7 Paul admitted, "My own behavior baffles me. For I find myself doing what I really loathe but not doing what I really really want to do....I often find that I have the will to do good, but not the power. That is, I don't accomplish the good I set out to do, and the evil I don't really want to do I find I am always doing."[5]

In the next chapter we'll look at possible misconceptions from the Scriptures that lead to perfectionism, as well as ways to get out of the perfectionist's trap.

Lord, I'm not perfect, but I know that doesn't make any difference to You. Help me realize that it shouldn't make that much difference to me, either.

Review the cycle of perfectionism at the end of the chapter. Do any of these characteristics sound familiar? If so, take heart and read on. There is a cure for the Avis Complex.

Notes
1. David A. Seamands, *Healing for Damaged Emotions* (Wheaton, IL: Victor Books, 1981), p. 79.
2. Dr. David Stoop, *Living with a Perfectionist* (Atlanta: Oliver Nelson, 1987), see especially chapter 2, "The World of the Perfectionist," pp. 31-45.
3. Fritz Ridenour, *Untying Your Knots* (Old Tappan: Fleming H. Revell Company, 1988), p. 112. Used by permission.
4. See Matthew 5:48, *Phillips.*
5. Romans 7:15,18-20, *Phillips.*

The Hopeless Pursuit of Perfection

1. "It's all or nothing. I must be perfect."

2. "There is nothing I can't do or accomplish."

3. "How did I get into this? I'll never be able to get it all done."

4. "It could have been better...I blew it again!"

5. "I am what I do...the only thing that counts is results—performance!"

6. "I'll try harder—I know I can do better than that!"

1. Trapped in dichotomous-thinking, the perfectionist believes that life is an all-or-nothing, either/or proposition. The perfectionist has the highest expectations, nothing will suffice but flawless achievement.

2. The drive for perfection translates into setting unrealistic or impossible goals. The perfectionist bites off far more than any human being can chew by setting too many goals at once or setting his or her sights so high there is no possible chance to succeed.

3. Because of unrealistic expectations and unattainable goals, the perfectionist feels overwhelmed and suffers the "hurdle effect." Looking into the future, all the perfectionist can see are problems, hurdles, and obstacles. The perfectionist lives in the future wondering how he or she will manage to "get it all done this time."

4. As you hurdle through life, you confront the M-and-M principle, which means you maximize your failures and minimize your success and achievements. Even if you do well, it could have been better. And if you fail or even make minor errors, you kick yourself for not being up to standard.

5. When you don't meet your unrealistic goals or aren't even happy with goals you do reach, you feel inadequate as a person. Your self-esteem suffers and your self-image diminishes. You believe that your worth as a person depends on your performance and results.

6. You develop an "Avis Complex"—the compulsion to try harder to "be better next time." This only results in more all-or-nothing thinking, more unrealistic impossible goals, more feeling overwhelmed.

CHAPTER NINETEEN

From Perfectionism to Excellence (In Several Rather Difficult Steps)

Lord, if I dig a pit for others,
Let me fall into it;
But if I dig it for myself
Give me sense enough to
walk around.
—Sherwood Wirt[1]

"Who will rescue me from this body of death? Thanks be to God—through Jesus Christ our Lord!"
—Romans 7:24,25

Is there a way out of the perfectionist trap? You may not be able to get rid of your perfectionism completely (at least I haven't), but there are ways to cope. One of the best I've found is "going back to the roots," in this case, my spiritual roots.

In *Discipleship Journal*, Lois Easley tells of always equating her performance with who she was during her growing up years. If she did well, great, but if she made a mistake, she writhed on the spit of perfectionism. Even after becoming a Christian and realizing that God loved her unconditionally, it was hard to break thought patterns that had formed over a lifetime.[2]

The apostle Paul had the same problem. Born of the tribe of Benjamin, a Pharisee of the Pharisees, Paul had obeyed the law with almost flawless precision (see Phil. 3:4-6). Ironically, he found living in Christ's love more difficult than jumping through legalistic hoops. Romans 7 catalogues his struggle against doing what he didn't want to do and not doing what he knew he should.

As chapter 7 ends, Paul cries out for help, asking for some kind of deliverance from his human nature—his body of death. With a sudden flash of insight, he continues, "Thanks be to God—through Jesus Christ our Lord!...Therefore, there is now no condemnation for those who are in Christ Jesus, because through Christ Jesus the law of the Spirit of life set me free from the law of sin and death" (Rom. 7:25, 8:1-2). It is as though Paul has to remember something he knows better than most—that God's acceptance of any believer has nothing to do with that believer's performance.

As Lois Easley began to understand her own perfectionism, she realized, "God's love for me has never been affected by my attempts—or lack of attempts—to earn it....He still loves me when my spiritual disciplines seem to be sadly lacking."[3]

If we want to try to distill the "no condemnation" theology of Romans 8:1 into everyday language, it might sound like this:

> Because I know Christ, God will not denounce or incriminate me. He will not attack, lash out, curse or revile me for my failures. He still loves me even though my house is a mess or my budget has succumbed to another shopping spree. He still loves me even though I have bungled an opportunity to witness to my neighbor. He still loves me even though I deliberately cut off that semi back at the interchange. He still loves me even though unkind words fell from my lips all over my family when I got home.

Paul doesn't use the word "grace" anywhere in Romans 7 or 8, but it is grace the he is talking about. The former Pharisee who prided himself in his perfection knows that the bottom line to grace is that God loves him even when he blows it.

This is a hard pill for any perfectionist to swallow. The perfectionist may readily admit, "Yes, I know all about Romans 8:1 and I agree with it in my head, but when I make mistakes, my stomach still keeps score."

I know exactly how that feels because I, too, tend to trust in my own performance rather than to trust in God. I have a habit of telling myself, "It all depends on me."

Of course, it all doesn't depend on me—or any of us. As hard as it may be for the perfectionist to understand, God's presence in his or her life is what counts, not "perfect" results or totally favorable circumstances. The rest of

Romans 8 outlines the victory that is possible through the power of the life-giving Spirit who dwells in every believer (see especially Rom. 8:2ff).

Through the power of the Holy Spirit, Paul learned to be content, whatever the circumstances (see Phil. 4:11).

The path from perfectionism to contentment lies in trusting God to make the best out of our good—and our not-so-good.

Furthermore, he said, "I can do all things through Christ who strengthens me" (Phil. 4:13, *NKJV*). What Paul didn't mean, however, is that you can do everything on an overloaded to-do list that three people couldn't handle in a month of Sundays. Kenneth Taylor's *Living Bible Paraphrased* brings out Paul's meaning best: "For I can do everything God asks me to with the help of Christ."

There is usually a vast difference between what God expects of us and what we expect of ourselves. Paul seemed to realize that there would always be a tension in the Christian's life and that's why he told his friends in Philippi: "Complete the salvation that God has given you with a proper sense of awe and responsibility. For it is God who is at work within you, giving you the will and the power to achieve his purpose" (Phil. 2:12,13, *Phillips*).

God joins with each believer to make an unbeatable team. That's what Jesus meant by telling us to take His yoke because it would be easy (see Matt. 11:29,30). A yoke is always built for two, not one, and when we share our load with Jesus, it has to be lighter. The path from perfectionism to contentment lies in trusting God to make the best out of our good—and our not-so-good. This may mean turning in a project even before it's as perfect as we'd like it to be. It may mean making a deadline rather than being late by pursuing the Holy Grail of Quality (i.e., perfectionism).

I admit all this is much easier said than accomplished. After all, there are standards and there are expectations, not only your own, but those of others. The cure for perfectionism is not sloppiness or shoddy work. Instead, seek excellence, which David Stoop defines as living in tune with your goals, seeking reasonable achievements through agreed-on objectives for yourself and others.[4]

What if the little voice comes back to remind us that Christ Himself said, "Be perfect, even as your Father in heaven is perfect"? When that happens I remind myself that Jesus wasn't talking about flawless performance. The word used for "perfect" in Matthew 5:48 means mature, complete or whole. To paraphrase Jesus' words, "Seek to grow, mature and become all God wants you to be."

What exactly is the difference between realistically seeking excellence and hopelessly pursuing perfection? To begin finding the answer for yourself, try these questions:

1. Am I striving to do my best, or be the best?
2. Do I tell myself I will or I should?
3. Am I motivated by a desire for success or a fear of failure?
4. Am I enjoying the process or am I focusing on the product, which must be perfect?
5. Am I setting a high standard to get the best for myself or am I trying to outdo everyone else?
6. Is life a challenge or is it a curse, crisis, or dogfight every day?

7. When I finish a job, do I feel accomplishment, acceptance, or fulfillment, or do I have a sense of disappointment, frustration, or even failure because it wasn't "as good as it could have been"?
8. Do I realize that nobody's perfect, or do I tell myself perfection is possible—especially mine?[5]

In each of the above questions, it's not too hard to tell the perfectionist from the seeker of excellence. Perfectionists follow a code they can never live up to; pursuers of excellence live by grace.

And that makes all the difference.

Lord, I am thankful that You are perfect, but I am even more thankful that You are gracious.

As you try to move from perfectionism to seeking excellence, remember:

Perfectionism sets impossible goals, excellence sets high standards within reach.

Perfectionism values "what I do," excellence values "who I am."

Perfectionism dwells on mistakes, excellence learns from them.

Perfectionism says, "I've got to be Number One." Excellence says, "I did my best and I'm satisfied."[6]

Notes
1. Sherwood E. Wirt, *Go Tell It and Other Poems* (Kansas City: Beacon Hill, 1979), p. 37. Used by permission.
2. Lois Easley, "Can a Perfectionist Be Content?" *Discipleship Journal*, Issue 42, 1987, p. 28.

3. Ibid., p. 28.
4. See David Stoop, *Living with a Perfectionist* (Old Tappan: Fleming H. Revell Company, 1987), p. 57.
5. Adapted from David Stoop, *Living with a Perfectionist* (Nashville: Oliver-Nelson Books, 1987), p. 59. Also quoted in Fritz Ridenour, *Untying Your Knots* (Old Tappan: Fleming H. Revell Company, 1988), p. 123.
6. Adapted from Kevin Leman, *The Birth Order Book* (Old Tappan, New Jersey: Fleming H. Revell Company, 1985), p. 70.

CHAPTER TWENTY

What Are You Doing Down Under the Gun?

Some men die by shrapnel
And some go down in flames,
But most men perish
inch by inch
In play at little games.[1]

"The procrastinator is wiser in his own eyes than seven men who answer discreetly."
—Proverbs 26:16 (paraphrased)[2]

Ensign Jones* was getting nervous. A storm was brewing and the prow of the huge man-of-war started to slice through ever rising white caps. The giant cannon, which was the ensign's responsibility, was lashed to the afterdeck. He had been assigned to oversee shipment of the giant gun to a fort several hundred miles away, and all had gone well on the first days of the voyage. But now he heard the captain tell the first mate, "Looks like we're in for a nasty blow. Have everything checked to be sure it's secure."

Ensign Jones immediately thought of the huge cannon and went aft to check it. As the huge ship pitched and rolled beneath his feet, he wondered if there were enough lines to hold the cannon during the storm. All seemed secure, but the giant gun weighed well over half a ton and if it ever got loose on the deck there would be chaos.

Deciding he'd put another line or two on the gun a little later, the ensign went below to grab a cup of hot soup and change into some dry clothes. The soup was extra good and the ensign stayed a little longer than he had intended. As he was downing the last of his bowl, he heard a strange rumbling above the rising whine of the storm above deck. Then there were shouts of alarm that turned into screams of panic.

Bounding topside, the ensign found the deck awash with huge waves and the cannon, which he had left "securely lashed down," running amuck! It had almost smashed through the starboard rail and into the sea, but a sudden roll of the ship reversed its direction and it came thundering back the other way, straight for the main mast where two sailors frantically worked to strike additional canvas to ride out the storm.

In seconds, the ensign saw the situation. The sailors

*The source of this supposedly true story is hard to pin down. The real name of the ensign is unknown.

were so busy they had no idea that disaster was bearing down on them. The huge gun would easily crush both men and probably bring down the main mast as well. There was no time to think; a shouted warning would only be lost in the howl of the gale. Acting on instinct, he

---

Heroic efforts at the last second are no substitute for being responsible for doing what's important now, not "later."

---

made one huge bound and threw himself under the iron wheels of the huge gun, to try to bring it to a halt.

The ensign's act of heroism worked. The gun ground to a halt, less than a foot from the sailors and the main mast. It also ground the ensign's legs into the deck, and he writhed in pain with multiple compound fractures. Somehow the two sailors lassoed the cannon with additional ropes and got it secured. Then they rushed Ensign Jones below for first aid.

A few days later, the ensign lay in sick bay, trying to recover from the horrible injuries that had made it necessary for the ship's surgeon to amputate his right leg just below the knee. The first mate came in and announced that the captain had assembled all hands and wanted the ensign on deck immediately.

With the help of two seamen carrying his stretcher, the ensign arrived topside, thinking, The Captain's probably going to give me a commendation for bravery.

With no preliminary comments, the captain read from a prepared statement, which catalogued the events the night of the storm and how the loose cannon had been stopped only by the sacrificial heroism of Ensign Jones. Noting that the ensign's bravery deserved highest honors, the captain then cited an even higher law of the sea: "For negligence in carrying out your primary responsibility to keep the cannon secured, you will be held under guard until we reach port, at which time you will be remanded to the authorities for court martial, with recommendations that you be executed for endangering this ship and its crew."

I can't be sure the above story is true. I found a brief version on a study guide sheet from a corporation seminar.[3] But it is a plausible illustration of why a lot of people, myself included, often complain of "being under the gun." The moral of the ensign's fate is plain: procrastinating doesn't pay. Heroic efforts at the last second are no substitute for being responsible for doing what's important now, not "later."

You won't find many people who disagree with the wisdom in "doing it now." But a lot of us simply don't follow through. Much of the human race is guilty of procrastination from time to time for any one of several reasons:

1. *Perfectionism can cause procrastinating.* This sounds like a contradiction at first, until you think about it. While perfectionists appear to be highly efficient and totally organized, they often procrastinate because they "know they won't be able to do it right anyway, so why start the project?" Finally, with the deadline closing in, the perfectionist roars into action with a cloud of dust, telling himself and everyone else, "I work better under pressure."

2. *Wanting to play it safe* is another reason many people procrastinate. We much prefer success to failure, as one motivational specialist discovered

when he made a trip to the Library of Congress to research the effects of disappointment and failure and how people bounce back from loss or misfortune. He found more than twelve hundred books on success and only seventeen on subjects like losing or failure.[4]

Fear of failure keeps some people procrastinating in the hope that if they wait long enough, perhaps the deadline (opportunity) will pass and they won't have to deal with it. That works sometimes, but in many cases the challenge or problem won't go away and then they really wind up "under the gun."

3. Perhaps the most common cause of procrastination, however, is *simple laziness.* The Bible calls it sloth and describes the slothful man (sluggard) like this:

> Do you see a man wise in his own eyes?
> There is more hope for a fool than for him.
> The slothful man says, "There is a lion in
>   the road!
> A fierce lion is in the streets!"
> As a door turns on its hinges,
> So does the slothful turn on his bed.
> The slothful man buries his hand in the bowl;
> It wearies him to bring it back to his mouth.
> The sluggard is wiser in his own eyes
> Than seven men who can answer sensibly
> (Prov. 26:12-16, *NKJV*).

The apostle Paul also had a few words of warning to sluggards, whom he called busybodies, warning them if they didn't work they shouldn't expect to eat (see 2 Thess. 3:10-12). Busybodies bustle about, creating the image of being overworked but they accomplish little. As someone has said, "When all is said and done, much is said and little is done."[5]

Whether we are perfectionists, play-it-safers, or just a little lazy, one of life's ironies is that the important things (like lashing down loose cannons) often fall into the "can do it later" category. We may think we can put it off for a few minutes, a few hours or a few days, but the bottom line is that we nudge a lot of things aside, telling ourselves, "I'll have more time soon," or "That will have to wait....I know it's important, but..." Another favorite excuse phrase is, "As soon as...":

> I will start playing catch with Johnny or teaching Susie how to bake cookies *as soon as* things slow down a bit at work.
>
> I'll go on that diet *as soon as* the holidays are over.
>
> We'll get the garage cleaned up *as soon as* we get back from vacation.
>
> We'll start having quiet time and praying for more than thirty seconds as soon as we get things under control around here.

The truth is, everyone procrastinates about something or in some area because we simply can't do everything "as soon as" we would like. We know the answer to "as soon as" is to "do it now." But like most simple truths, doing it now is never easy to practice. Then there is also the problem of deciding what needs doing now first (i.e., priorities). The answer to having enough time and feeling less hassled and pressured lies in becoming "proactive." As we will see, a rule of life is: "Act or be acted upon." It's your choice—and the way out from under the gun.

———————

Lord, I'm tired of being under the gun. Help me to take a hard look at why I wind up there so often.

———————

Take the "Are You a Procrastinator?" quiz on the following pages. If it reveals procrastination is a problem for you, take inventory: What tasks or actions are you putting off and why?

"Are You a Procrastinator?"

If procrastinating is a problem for you, it can help explain why you never have enough time and always seems to be running behind. The following is a little quiz I put together to help locate causes of procrastination. There is no scoring system. But if even a few yeses or "often true's" pop up, procrastination is probably part of your rat race syndrome.

1. When faced with big or important tasks, do I stall by reorganizing my desk, cleaning my cupboards, straightening files, going shopping?
2. Does change, risk or a new situation cause me concern, even fear?
3. When faced with difficult or unpleasant situations do I tend to get headaches or feel ill?
4. Do I try to get out of unpleasant tasks by delaying, criticizing, or complaining until someone else does it?
5. Do I make plans and to-do lists but have difficulty following through on them?
6. Am I staying in a job that I don't really like and find unfulfilling and unchallenging?
7. Do I put off tough jobs and wait for a "better time" instead of taking constructive steps toward solutions?
8. Do I put off dieting, quitting smoking, or that trip to the drug-treatment center by saying, "I'll quit when I'm ready"?
9. Do I put off those menial chores that I really want to get done but never do, like cleaning the garage, painting the lawn furniture, etc.?
10. Do I tend to avoid confrontations with friends, spouse, sales people?

11. Do I put off spending a special day or even a special few minutes with my children because I am "too busy"?

12. Do I use sleep or "being tired" as an excuse for putting things off?

13. Do I find myself being bored a great deal of the time?

14. Do I put off doing beneficial things for myself (i.e., an exercise program, a day alone, etc.) because I "live for my family"?[6]

Notes

1. Robert D. Abrahams, "The Night They Burned Shanghai," quoted in Edwin C. Bliss's *Doing It Now* (New York: Charles Scribner's Sons, 1938).
2. The *NIV* translation of this verse reads: "The sluggard is wiser in his own eyes than seven men who answer discreetly." Procrastinators and sluggards have similar problems.
3. The study guide sheet containing the "Under the Gun" story was developed by the Main Event Management Corporation of Sacramento, California. Origin of the story is unknown.
4. See Gerhard Gschwandtner and Laura B. Gschwandtner, *Super Sellers: Portraits of Success from Personal Selling Power* (Amacom, American Management Assn., 1986), p. 8.
5. Dr. Robert Anthony, *Think*, (New York: Berkley Publishing Group, 1987).
6. See Fritz Ridenour, *Untying Your Knots* (Old Tappan: Fleming H. Revell Company, 1988), pp. 91-92. Used by permission.

CHAPTER TWENTY-ONE

"Mean to" Don't Pick No Cotton!

He slept beneath the moon,
He basked beneath the sun;
He lived a life of going-to-do
And died with nothing done.
—James Albery[1]

"A little sleep, a little slumber, a little folding of the hands to rest—and poverty will come on you like a bandit."
—Proverbs 6:10,11

All right, suppose you took the quiz in the previous chapter and are willing to confess to procrastinating at least now and then. Mostly then, of course. What can you do about it? Already we are flirting with the solution to procrastination—*doing* something—preferably now, not later.

If you are a procrastinator and really want to change, it will help to see the difference in being proactive rather than remaining reactive. Procrastinators are reactive, meaning *they wait for life to act upon them.* They may have values and principles for living but they leave them on the back shelf of their minds and operate according to their feelings instead. And their favorite feeling is "I just don't feel like it right now."

For procrastinators, this bit of bumper sticker wisdom is all too true:

IF IT WEREN'T FOR THE LAST MINUTE,
NOTHING WOULD EVER GET DONE!

In sharp contrast to procrastinators, proactivists act now instead of at the last minute. They take responsibility for their lives and make decisions based on their values and principles. Their feelings don't control them; instead their goals, commitments and sense of being responsible all drive them forward.

It is no coincidence that, when Stephen Covey wrote *The Seven Habits of Highly Effective People*, he led off with "Habit 1: Being Proactive." The proactive person realizes that responsibility refers to the ability to choose your own response. According to Covey, highly proactive people:

...do not blame circumstances, conditions, or conditioning for their behavior. Their behavior is a product of their own conscious choice based on values, rather than a product of their conditions, based on feeling....The ability to subordinate the impulse to a value is the essence of the proactive person. Reactive people are driven by feelings, by circumstances, by conditions, by their environment. Proactive people are driven by values—carefully thought about, selected and internalized values.[2]

The road to reactive living is paved with good intentions, but the proactive person doesn't just "intend"—he or she thinks it through and gets it done.

To use proactivity to do away with procrastination, work on these areas:

1. *Listen to your own language.* Is it essentially proactive or reactive? The reactive procrastinator says:

"I meant to do it but I forgot."

"I'd like to do it, but I just don't have time right now."

"I don't see how I can do it—there is just nothing I can do about it."

"I know I put things off, but that's just the way I am."

To turn that kind of reactive talk into proactive language takes a different attitude. Yes, painful as it sounds, it requires change. Proactivists would tell their procrastinating side:

"I'll do this before I leave for lunch."

"This needs doing—I'll make time for it today."

"This may take some effort—what are my options?"

"It would be nice to goof off, but I can choose to be responsible."

You can find plenty of reactive examples in Scripture, especially the proverbs written by King Solomon who had a lot to say to sluggards—the slothful types who make procrastination a way of life. The sluggard's language is always reactive. For example, the sluggard says, "Oh, for just a little more sleep, a little more slumber, a little folding of my hands to rest and then I'll get going" (see Prov. 6:10).

The sluggard becomes so reactive in his approach to life that he will "bury his hand in the dish," and not even have energy to bring it back up to his mouth (see Prov. 19:24). He just feels too tired. Governed by his feelings, the sluggard doesn't plow his ground and do his planting when he is supposed to. Is it any wonder at harvest time he finds nothing? (See Prov. 20:4.)

The reactive person desires, wishes, craves and wants, but nothing much happens because he or she refuses to work (see Prov. 21:25). Instead, the reactive person finds solace in cute little slogans like:

HOUSEWORK ROTS THE MIND

The road to reactive living is paved with good intentions, but the proactive person doesn't just "intend"—he or she thinks it through and gets it done. Separating us from chickens, rabbits and horses is our built-in capacity to think and make rational choices. When we give up that privilege, we become reactive and can easily slip into all kinds of negative behavior, including procrastination.

2. Work on "be" instead of "have." The reactive person

focuses on all the circumstances and conditions that give him many of his concerns, but about which he can do very little. He winds up blaming other people or the situation for his plight.

The favorite word of the reactive procrastinator is "have" or "had." He hopes to have his bills paid soon. He wishes he had a wife who was easier to get along with. She wishes she had a more patient husband.

The reactive procrastinator says, "If only I had that degree in business, I could move up the ladder much quicker," or "If I could just have more time for me, I might be able to relax."

The favorite word of the proactive person is "be." Instead of worrying about having the bills paid, the proactivist says, "I can be more economical here and have more money to pay those bills." Instead of murmuring about having a spouse who isn't very agreeable, the proactivist says, "I can be kinder and more loving and build my spouse up instead of complaining."

Instead of wishing for a degree, the proactivist says, "I'll be a CPA in two more semesters." Instead of complaining about lack of time, the proactivist organizes his schedule around being busy for several hours, then taking a brief break before going at it again.

Examples of proactive people are all over the Bible. When Nehemiah led a group of Israelites back from exile to Jerusalem to rebuild the city's walls, he faced all kinds of problems and a great deal of "things that needed doing." Instead of worrying about what he had or didn't have (for example, more friendly neighbors), Nehemiah focused on being organized, diligent and persistent. Result? The wall was rebuilt in fifty-two days (see Neh. 6:15).

One of the most proactive people in the New Testament was Paul the Apostle. Instead of saying, "If only we had more converts to Christianity," Paul focused on being faithful, committed and persistent, and succeeded in spreading the gospel throughout the then known world. When Paul received a vision of a man from Macedonia begging him to come and help, he didn't say, "I think we'd better have a committee meeting and study this further." Paul was a man of prayer, but prayer always spurred him to action and being what he knew God wanted him to be.

3. Use Action TNT. One of the most proactive people I have ever met is Denis Waitley, who holds a Ph.D. in human behavior and is known throughout the world for his seminars and workshops on high level performance and personal development. Millions have heard his voice on *The Psychology of Winning*, the best-selling audiocassette album of all time.

One of the best things about Denis is that he doesn't push gaining power, authority, money, beauty, influence or all the other goodies many success hucksters try to sell. Instead, he concentrates on helping people learn to live successfully by being the best they can be, trusting in their Creator and the gifts He has given them. Concerning procrastination, Denis says:

> After years of study and some painful experiences of my own, I'm convinced that people often procrastinate and resist change because they are afraid of the perceived "cost" of success. And the costs are there: taking responsibility to change old habits; distancing yourself from a peer group that isn't helping you succeed; leading yourself and others down an unfamiliar path; working more and delaying your own gratification as you work hard to reach your goals; and, perhaps, the toughest cost

of all, facing criticism and jealousy of friends, family and business associates.

To become a winner across the board in life, you must assert your options to take responsibility for making the best use of what you have—your mind, your talents, your developed ability, and that precious commodity called "the time we have to spend on living...." You are the only one who can steal your own time, talent and accomplishments. The choice is yours.[3]

Denis's choices focus on being and doing. Two simple rhymes he often uses in seminars are:

IF IT'S TO BE IT'S UP TO ME

STOP STEWING AND START DOING

Denis is fond of the phrase, "Action TNT" which means "Action Today, Not Tomorrow." He also likes to say, "It's very difficult to be active and depressed at the same time."

Edwin Bliss is a time management specialist who has held many anti-procrastination seminars and has also written the best-seller, *Getting Things Done*. Over the years, he has picked up many mottos and slogans to help procrastinators break their habit.[4] A few samples:

- Get the now habit.
- Tomorrow is never.
- Life is leaking through your fingers.
  There's a time to work
  And a time to play...
  It's time to work.

And one of my favorites turned out to be the title of this chapter:

"MEAN TO" DON'T PICK NO COTTON!

I think the apostle Paul would have especially liked that one. The only way to pick cotton or do anything else is to get out and get at it. In Philippians 2:12,13, Paul urges us to work out our salvation with fear and trembling because God is working in us. A procrastinator's paraphrase of these verses might put it this way:

> You're saved by grace, but you can't grow and change without some effort. Do what needs doing now and God will do the rest.

Lord, wherever I need it, please give me
a jump start—now.

Use these simple techniques to put Action TNT into practice:

Take a few minutes to write down what you've been putting off. Then immediately do one of the tasks that you've written down. Instead of using your energy to make excuses (reactive thinking), put that energy into proactive accomplishment.

Set a specific time to get started on a project that you've been putting off. Maybe you can start next Thursday during thirty minutes over lunch hour. The point is, start, and don't worry about being perfect. What you're after is making a quality effort and let the results fall where they may.

Maybe what you're putting off involves another person and what you really need to do is communicate. Your reasons for procrastinating may suddenly vanish.

If you fear that taking action may cause trouble or inconvenience, ask yourself, "What is the worst thing that could happen if I did this today?" Often, the worst thing that could happen is a minor inconvenience, and that would be well worth getting something accomplished.

Finally, picture how you'll feel when that long put-off project is completed. The pressure, self-doubt and anxiety will be gone. That alone should get you going.[5]

Notes
1. James Albery, "Epitaph Written for Himself," *Home Book of Quotations* (New York: Dodd, Mead, 1964).
2. Stephen Covey, *The Seven Habits of Highly Effective People* (New York: Simon and Schuster, 1989), pp. 71,72.
3. From Denis Waitley, *Seasons of Success*, audiocassette album (New York: McGraw Hill, 1986). Used by permission.
4. Quoted by Edwin Bliss, *Doing It Now* (New York: Bantam Books, 1984), pp. 169-172.
5. Adapted from Denis Waitley, *Seasons of Success,* audiocassette album. Used by permission.

CHAPTER TWENTY-TWO

Strategy for Living: To Get Going, Set Some Goals

"If you don't know what direction to take, you haven't acknowledged where you are."
—Dr. Robert Anthony[1]

"Live life, then, with a due sense of responsibility....Make the best use of your time."
—Ephesians 5:15,16 (*Phillips*)

What is the best conference or seminar you ever attended? For me it's a toss-up between a time management package conducted by Ed Dayton and Ted Engstrom and a Family Life conference offered by Dennis Rainey and his excellent supporting staff of speakers and leaders.

From Dayton and Engstrom I learned that the key to getting control of time is setting goals, deciding on priorities and making your plans. With Dennis Rainey, I was reminded—after thirty-six years, three children and four grandchildren—that the key to a good marriage is setting aside time to communicate with each other. In other words, marriage takes goals, priorities and planning, too!

Dayton and Engstrom have put their seminar into a book, appropriately called *Strategy for Living*. They make it clear at the start that they are not prescribing a formula for time management, but a strategy, which they state in one brief sentence:

Set your goals,
Establish your priorities,
Work out plans to reach those goals,
And then measure life and your days against those goals.

Perhaps no other passage of Scripture sums up this strategy better than the *Phillips* translation of Ephesians 5:15,16:

Live life, then, with a due sense of responsibility,not as men who do not know the meaning of life but as those who do. Make the best use ofyour time, despite all the evils of these days.

Dayton and Engstrom's strategy for living starts appropriately enough with the need to set goals. With goals, you get somewhere, without them you spin your wheels. With goals, you know where you're going and what you want to accomplish; without them, you are an unguided missile, aimed at nothing and sure to hit it.

Despite the obvious value of goals, some people shy away from setting them, reasoning that God would not approve. Somehow they feel that setting a goal would be trespassing on the Holy Spirit's sovereign territory. They prefer to "go with the flow" and "let God lead." After all, doesn't Psalm 31:15 say our times are in God's hands? And what about James 4:13,14 and its warning against saying you'll do this thing or that today or tomorrow when you really don't know what will happen?

Actually, read in their total context, both of these passages acknowledge the sovereign care and rule of God but they certainly don't rule out setting goals. We are as free to set goals and lay plans as we are to think, trust and believe.

Every time we set a goal, we are making a statement of faith. As the writer of Hebrews said, "Faith means that we have full confidence in the things we hope for" (Heb. 11:1, *Phillips*). Our goals describe what we hope will happen in the future, "the Lord willing" (see Jas. 4:15).

Another common problem is to confuse purposes with goals. Dayton and Engstrom define a purpose as "an aim or direction, something which we want to achieve, but something which is not necessarily measurable." Their definition of a goal is: "a future event which we believe is both accomplishable and measurable. Measurable in terms of what is to be done and how long it takes to do it."[2]

For example, you might decide your purpose is to "become more loving and effective in my daily work or routine." How can you reduce this broad purpose to some specific goals that are measurable? To become more loving, you might decide to spend at least ten or fifteen minutes praying for people and then dropping them an encouraging note or calling them. Or you might decide to spend at least thirty minutes a day reading a book that will help you become more effective in your job. Another specific goal to achieve your purpose could be: "Say or do something loving or encouraging toward my clients or my fellow workers (or members of my family) at least once each day."

A good goal is always written with the end result in mind. It usually has a time limit and is definite as to what you expect you will do. A good goal is practical and usually limited to one important statement. One reason why we often find our time frittering away and nothing much getting accomplished is that we dream about purposes rather than set goals and then actually go after them.

For example, "Having more time to spend with my family" is not a goal, it is a purpose. If you want to turn that purpose into reality, you have to set a goal such as: "Leave work by 5:00 P.M. at least three nights a week and be home by 6:00 in time for dinner."

Or, another way of carving out time for your family would be setting a goal like: "Take only one committee position or teaching responsibility at church this year." Then, when the other invitations come, you can say, "Sorry, I've already taken on teaching a Bible study and that's it for right now."

One of the best ways to set a goal and accomplish it is to "act as if you had reached this goal already."[3] For example, if you have set a goal of leaving the office by 5:00 at least three days each week in order to be home in time for dinner, start acting as if you've already reached your goal, and you will have a tremendous psychological advantage.

No last second emergency or "one more thing that I ought to do" will hold you back.

In his letters to his son, Lord Chesterfield admonished him not to be idle, lazy or procrastinating, summing up his advice in the well-known motto, "Never put off until tomorrow what you can do today." That's good advice if you simply aren't getting much done at all and need to break strong procrastination habits. On the other hand, if

---

Without goals, you can easily lose control of your time and schedule and slip into the ranks of the disorganized.

---

your specific goal is to leave work on time to spend the evening with your family, you would want to amend Lord Chesterfield's advice to say: "Never put off until tomorrow the goal you have set to reach today," which, in this case, means getting home for dinner at 6:00, not dragging in for the 9:00 o'clock news.

Acting as if you've reached your goal takes perseverance. As Josh Billings put it: "Be like a postage stamp—stick to one thing until you get there."

One of the greatest advantages of goal setting is that goals help you become organized. Without goals, you can easily lose control of your time and schedule and slip into the ranks of the disorganized.

In *Ordering Your Private World*, Gordon MacDonald lists several warning signs that help him become aware he's slipping into disorganization: his desk gets overly cluttered—and so does his car because he's failing to take time to keep it clean and properly serviced. He starts to miss appointments and deadlines and fails to answer telephone messages. Next he finds himself doing a lot of "time burning" (i.e., procrastinating) and unproductive tasks. The quality of his personal relationships also goes down (no meaningful conversations with wife or children) and he begins to get irritable, not liking himself, his job or his world.[4]

MacDonald also observes that disorganized Christians rarely have time for drawing closer to God. They know they should set aside regular periods for Bible study, prayer and quiet reflection on what God is telling them, but somehow it doesn't happen. Some urgent task always seems to interfere—for example, getting to work on time because of getting up late.

Many people live under the "tyranny of the urgent," while neglecting the truly important things. Taking time for knowing God better may be a goal, but is it a priority? Sorting out priorities is an art in itself as we will see in the next chapter.

Lord, give me wisdom to set goals that glorify You.

Write down three short-range spiritual goals to be accomplished in the next thirty days. Then evaluate each goal by asking yourself:

1. Is this goal specific?
2. Does this goal have some kind of time limit or target date?
3. Is this goal realistic and achievable?

Notes

1. Dr. Robert Anthony, *Think* (New York: Berkley Publishing Group, 1987).
2. Edward R. Dayton, Ted W. Engstrom, *Strategy for Living* (Ventura: Regal Books, 1976), p. 49.
3. Dayton and Engstrom, *Strategy for Living*, p. 56.
4. See Gordon MacDonald, *Ordering Your Private World* (Atlanta: Oliver Nelson, 1985), pp. 66,67.

CHAPTER TWENTY-THREE

Strategy for Living: Prioritize or Spin Your Wheels?

"Urgent matters are usually visible....They're usually right in front of us and often they are easy, pleasant, fun to do, but so often they are unimportant!"

—Stephen Covey[1]

"He that hath no rule over his own spirit is like a city that is broken down, and without walls."

—Proverbs 25:28 (*KJV*)

In order to reach a goal, it must become a true priority. If getting home on time for dinner with your family is a priority, practically nothing will stand in its way. That's not to say that an absolute crusher crisis might not cause a problem, but something of that magnitude should be rare. (If it isn't, maybe you should be looking for a different job—see chapter 26.)

The everyday, last second "emergencies" are often false alarms that can keep you at the office another hour or two. If fighting those kinds of fires is more important than getting home to spend time with your family, your family will come off second best.

Unfortunately, it isn't a simple matter of working on only one goal and making it a priority. Life seems to be filled with goals of all kinds—short range, intermediate and even long range. How do we sort them out? Ed Dayton and Ted Engstrom (*Strategy for Living*) observe: "In one sense, all priority questions are 'When?' questions. We are trying to decide what to do next and what to do after that. The least important things we will never get around to."[2]

Perhaps, like me, you have studied the various systems that can help you "put first things first." One of the most basic is the A-B-C approach.[3]

The basic idea is to take your to-do list and rate each item (goal) as follows:

A = "must do"
B = "should do"
C = "can do."

If you have trouble sorting out your to-do list, Dayton and Engstrom suggest that you go through all the items and decide which goals should be labeled *A*. Then go back through the list and label anything you think is a *B*. Anything left would automatically fall into the *C* category.[4]

As good as this system is, using it doesn't mean that you're out of the woods. If your life is anything like mine, you wind up with a lot of *A*'s, a few *B*'s and very few *C*'s. Sometimes everything seems to fall into the "must do" category. That's exactly why the "tyranny of the urgent" seems to take over and run your life.

Almost twenty years ago, Charles Hummel wrote a little booklet that opened with the question, "Have you ever wished for a thirty-four-hour day?" In *Tyranny of the Urgent*, Hummel speculated that an extra ten hours would help us with all our unfinished tasks—the unanswered letters, the unvisited friends, the unread books, the unmowed lawn, the unsewn dress and the unshopped groceries. That to-do list is never done and, as Hummel says, "We desperately need relief."[5]

Hummel was prompted to write his little booklet when the manager of a cotton mill told him, "Your greatest danger is letting the urgent things crowd out the important." All of us, says Hummel, live in a constant tension between the urgent and the important, but unfortunately the important tasks are often put off.

The "urgent things" press in each day: getting up, packing lunches, getting the children off to school, getting to work ourselves, stopping to shop or pick up the cleaning, paying the monthly bills, fixing meals, mending clothes, mowing lawns, the list is endless. But while we're taking care of all those urgent "can't wait" matters, the important things go undone.

And just exactly what is "important"? Each of us has his or her own list, but a few examples could be:

- Writing or phoning a friend you haven't contacted in several years;
- Getting that report that's due in six weeks started;

- Organizing the earthquake preparedness kit...or taking that course in CPR;
- Developing a consistent, disciplined prayer life;
- Developing *any* discipline that makes life a little simpler, more efficient or God-glorifying;
- Quit smoking (or overeating, or other addictive behavior).

There are just as many important tasks as there are urgent ones, but the important goals often get bumped aside again and again, until a deadline or crisis suddenly shoves them into the spotlight of urgency. That report that was due six weeks ago is due tomorrow. *Now* it becomes urgent. That survival kit that you should have prepared for the next earthquake (or tornado or hurricane), wasn't done and now that disaster has struck, there you sit with your family, in the dark with no food or water.

Down through the centuries, the urgent has always shouldered aside the important, and during today's time famine, the problem is getting worse, not better. The important goes undone and we realize it too late. As someone said, "To think too long about doing a thing often becomes its undoing."[6]

Go back for a moment to the A-B-C approach to prioritizing. Keep in mind that *A* items are "must do," *B* items are "should do," and *C* items are "can do." If the Tyrant Urgent is running your life, you may label some of your goals as *A* priority, but then you slip them over to *B* or *C* because they don't seem "that urgent" at the moment.

To reach any goal, it must become an A priority in your life. If you want to spend more time in Bible study or prayer, more time with your family, or more time working out, each of these goals must be stated in specific terms and then labeled with a big red *A* for "must do." The minute you let a goal slip into "should do" status, you are really saying that goal doesn't make quite that much difference, or at best it has become less important.

Learning to live out your priorities is a lifetime task and no one ever gets to the point where it's easy. Prioritizing means constantly making decisions. In their time

---

To prioritize is to decide. But when you fail to prioritize, you make a decision not to decide.

---

management seminars, Ed Dayton and Ted Engstrom love to tell the story of the crusty old bank president who was headed for retirement. His successor, a fast rising young executive, came in for some advice and asked him, "What would you say is the key to your success?"

The veteran banker replied, "Young man, two words: 'Good decisions!'"

"Thank you very much, Sir. But how does one make good decisions?" asked the younger man.

"One word, young man: 'Experience!'"

"But how does one get experience?"

"Two words, young man: 'Bad decisions!'"[7]

A few years ago, the following cryptic observation became a poster and then a bumper sticker:[8]

NOT TO DECIDE
IS TO DECIDE!

Keep these simple lines in mind when prioritizing. To

prioritize is to decide. But when you fail to prioritize, you make a decision *not to decide.* The important seldom has a chance and the urgent dominates your life and schedule.

Like the ten bridesmaids in Jesus' parable, you can find yourself "out of oil" with no time to get more, left on the outside looking in. This graphic story, told in Matthew 25, dramatizes the danger in neglecting the important because you happen to be busy with the "urgent."

As the story goes, five of the bridesmaids were wise and brought extra oil for the lamps, but five were foolish and forgot. All ten of them arrived at the home of the bride where they spent busy hours helping her. Their dresses, getting their hair just right, and a dozen other details crowded in and the five foolish girls forgot (or put off) a very important item: getting extra oil for their lamps.

Why was this extra oil so important? Because there would be a good chance that the procession to the bride-groom's home might be held at night, and without oil to keep their lamps brightly burning, they could not make their way along the dark and sometimes dangerous path.

Eventually, night fell and everyone grew weary and decided to take a nap. Around midnight a cry was heard: "The bridegroom is coming!" Down the path he came to greet his bride, and then the procession would return to the bridegroom's home for the ceremony, with everyone light-ing his way along the path with his own lamp or torch.

Five of the bridesmaids realized that they didn't have enough oil to get very far. And the other five bridesmaids, who had been wise enough to bring some extra oil, couldn't spare any or they would have wound up in the dark, as well. So, the five foolish bridesmaids dashed to a nearby village, where they awakened an oil merchant and quickly bought some oil in haste and confusion.

Meanwhile, the wedding procession had wound its

way up the path to the bridegroom's home. By the time the five foolish bridesmaids got there, the door was shut, and when he heard their pleading calls, the bridegroom told them to "Go away" because it was too late.

According to Jewish tradition, the bridegroom's attitude was not unusual. In middle class and wealthier homes, this was often the case. If you came to the wedding late, you missed it all and could not attend.

It's true that Jesus didn't tell this parable to warn primarily against procrastinating. His primary message concerned being ready for His return. Still, there are some universal principles we can apply to the busy days that fill our lives. One obvious truth is we must always be ready for what life may bring. That means taking time to do the important before tackling the urgent. Seen in this light, the daily quiet time becomes much more than a nice little exercise that Christians should get in if they possibly can each day. In *Tyranny of the Urgent,* Charles Hummel writes:

> Over the years the greatest continuing struggle in the Christian life is the effort to make adequate time for daily waiting on God, weekly inventory and monthly planning. Since this time for receiving marching orders is so important, Satan will do everything he can to squeeze it out. Yet we know from experience that only by this means can we escape the tyranny of the urgent. This is how Jesus succeeded. He did not finish all the urgent tasks in Palestine, or all the things He would have liked to do, but He did finish the work which God gave Him.[9]

When Lloyd Ogilvie sits down to breakfast with his wife, she often asks him how he feels about the coming challenges for the day. He answers with the motto of a Highland regiment in his native Scotland: "Ready, Aye, Ready!"

Ogilvie wants that motto to be true every day of his life because he wants to be ready for everything—the opportunities and serendipities, as well as the problems and hassles. But he knows that's not possible unless he meets with the Lord first on each new day. As he writes:

"He gives the day and He will show the way....We don't know what any day will bring. To be 'Ready, Aye, Ready' for life's surprises is demanding. It means being in good spiritual condition, with our prayer muscles well-exercised."[10]

Your day is bound to include plenty of "urgent." To be "Ready, Aye, Ready," be sure to include the important!

Lord, please prepare me for what You have prepared this day.
Help me deal with the urgent, because I have also done
the important.

Make your own list of what is urgent in your life right now and what should be important (or more important). What are you letting go because you are simply too busy with rush jobs or even the regular routine? How can you open up time to do more of the important and get the urgent under control? What do you have to give up and what must you start to include?

Notes
1. Stephen Covey, *The Seven Habits of Highly Effective People* (New York: Simon and Schuster, 1989), p. 151.
2. Ed Dayton and Ted Engstrom, *Strategy for Living* (Ventura: Regal Books, 1976), p. 66.
3. See especially, Alan Laekin, *How to Get Control of Your Time and Your Life* (New York: Peter H. Wyden, Inc., 1973), chapter 4ff; also *Strategy for Living,*

Ed Dayton and Ted Engstrom, (Ventura: Regal Books, 1976), chapter 7.

4. Dayton and Engstrom, p. 7.
5. Charles E. Hummel, *Tyranny of the Urgent* (Downers Grove: InterVarsity Christian Fellowship, 1971), p. 3.
6. Eva Young, quoted in "Pocket Pal" for 1990 (Maywood, NJ: Myron Manufacturing Corp., © 1988).
7. This story is told by Edward R. Dayton, *Tools for Time Management* (Grand Rapids: Zondervan Publishing Company, 1974).
8. Credited to theologian Harvey Cox.
9. Charles E. Hummel, *Tyranny of the Urgent*, p. 14.
10. Lloyd Ogilvie, *Autobiography of God* (Ventura: Regal Books, 1979), p. 282.

CHAPTER TWENTY-FOUR

Strategy for Living: Do You Have a Plan?

"Half the unhappiness in the world is due to the failure of plans which were unreasonable or impossible; the other half is due to making no plans at all."[1]

"May he give you the desire of your heart and make all your plans succeed."
—Psalm 20:4

Planning is the final piece of the strategy for living puzzle. You can set your goals and you can choose your priorities, but unless you plan how you will reach those goals, you will waste a lot of time and energy.

In a sense, when you make your plans you are taking your first steps of action to reach your goals. The advantages of planning are so obvious, you would think more people would plan more often, or at least more carefully, to accomplish their objectives. For example:

Planning almost always saves time.

A better plan saves making two trips. A better plan anticipates the need for more material, or needing more time to accomplish what you are trying to do.

Planning can mean doing the job right the first time instead of flying by the seat of your pants and then having to go back and redo most of it.

If planning is to be of real use to you, however, you must always make plans that can be changed. Some people find it hard to be flexible in the area of their plans. They live by the credo: "We said we were going to do this, now let's stick to it." Solomon himself said, however, "It is pleasant to see plans develop. That is why fools refuse to give them up even when they are wrong" (Prov. 13:19, TLB).

Just how can you make good plans—the kind that are practical, reasonable, flexible and most effective? If planning is sometimes frustrating for you, try the principle of "helping and hindering forces," which works like this:

1. State the present situation—your problem, your need—whatever it is you feel should be done.
2. State your goal—what you hope to do about the problem or need.
3. State the helping forces that can move you toward your goal.

4. State the hindering forces that will prevent or impede you from reaching your goal.
5. Put down some steps you plan to take toward your goal. These steps will, in effect, be the heart of your plan.

Suppose your present situation finds you having not enough uninterrupted time with your spouse. You seldom

---

With a strategy for living, you will always have time to do what God wants you to do.

---

get a chance to talk and share, so, you set a new goal: to spend two hours a week alone with your spouse.

Next, you list the helping forces that can move you toward that goal. In this case, it could be your desire to be with your spouse, a strong need to share certain feelings about how your marriage is going, or you may be worried about drifting in opposite directions.

List the hindering forces next. What might prevent you from moving toward your goal? If you have children, that's always a key problem because they have many needs and often interrupt in one way or another. Perhaps you and your spouse have conflicting schedules. And then there is always that old favorite, "Not enough time." This last "hindering force" is really a cop-out. There is enough time. You just have to plan to find it.

So, what steps can you take to reach your goal of spending two hours a week alone with your spouse? First, you might discuss what the two of you would like to do during this two-hour period. Suppose you decide that you will have lunch or dinner together at least once a week and, to be specific, you will make it Wednesdays.

So, put the date on your calendar, but don't stop there. Be sure to do everything you can to "protect the time." Don't let the tyranny of the urgent tempt you into calling, "Sorry, Honey, but I don't think I can make it." If reaching that goal of spending more time together is really top priority, you will plan to make it happen.

The final step in your strategy for living is what Dayton and Engstrom call, "Living all of life."

Living is a process of putting our goals, priorities and plans into daily action and then taking time to take stock. In Paul's words, "Press toward the mark for the prize of the high calling," but always ask yourself, "How am I doing? Are my goals reachable, or do I need to redefine them?" It's far better to reach a do-able goal than to be continually frustrated by one that always seems out of reach.

Diagram A depicts the Strategy for Living as a clockwise circle. Begin at the top at 12:00 and set your goals. Move toward 3:00 by deciding on your priorities, and as you come to 6:00, you start doing your planning for the action you intend to take. At 9:00 you are doing your living, and as you move back toward 12:00, you need to do your evaluating, taking stock on just how it's going, what's working, and what needs to be redefined, restructured.

Then, from what you've learned, you can set new goals, which will lead to the strengthening of certain priorities and perhaps setting new ones. Then there will be more planning, more living, and more learning. And that is life—living it with the right sense of responsibility and priorities because you know its meaning and purpose.

You may not be able to get it all done, but you can get

GOALS
Use what you have decided...
what it is God wants you to be
and to do.

PLANNING
Analyze the best way to reach
your goals.

PRIORITIES
Discover which goals are
more important.

LIVING
Start working toward your
goals according to you plans.

Diagram A

done what really matters. "Commit to the Lord whatever you do, and your plans will succeed" (Prov. 16:3).

In the words of Michel Quoist, "Time is a gift of God and He will demand of us an exact accounting of it. But be at peace: God doesn't give us a job to do without at the same time giving us the means to accomplish it."[2] With a strategy for living, you will always have time to do what God wants you to do.

———

*Lord, I commit my hopes and dreams and daily routine to
You. I want my plans to fit into Your plan.*

———

Following are some questions to take inventory on how you are using your time and living your life.

What areas of time usage do I need to improve?

What part does goal setting play in my life?

How good am I really at choosing priorities and making them real priorities?

Do I make good plans far enough in advance?

Do I operate with an organized schedule?

Am I overcommitted—involved in too many outside activities, too much running, too many bases to cover?

Do I have trouble saying no?

Am I hurting myself by the way I use my time? If so, how?

Am I hurting others by the way I use my time? If so, how?

Does my relationship with God affect my use of time? In what way?

Does my use of time glorify God? In what way?

Step 1 Present Situation	Step 2 My Goal	Step 3 Forces Helping	Step 4 Forces Hindering	Step 5 Steps to Goal

Notes
1. Adapted from a quote by Edgar Watson Howe, Eleanor Doan, Editor, *Speaker's Source Book* (Grand Rapids, MI: Zondervan Publishing House, 1960), p. 189.
2. Quoted by Robert Banks, *The Tyranny of Time* (Downers Grove: InterVarsity Press, 1983), p. 231.

CHAPTER TWENTY-FIVE

Spending Quality Time Means Spending Quantity Time!

What kind of memories will your children have of you? Will they remember a father who spent time with them, played with them, laughed with them? Or will they think of you as someone who was preoccupied with work, unfinished projects, or a hobby?

—Dennis Rainey[1]

"Sons are a heritage from the Lord, children a reward from him."

—Psalm 127:3

One of the most insidiously dangerous myths created by the time famine is the concept of saving "quality time" for your loved ones or other important people in your life. Whoever coined this glib phrase meant well, I suppose. After all, the idea is to face the fact that schedules are packed, deadlines are everywhere and time is short, even nonexistent. Because you can't spend much time with your spouse or your child or an elderly parent or friend, you settle for shorter periods of "quality" time, during which, theoretically, you are supposedly more focused and communicative.

Quality time sounds good, but I'm skeptical. So is Robert Banks who observes in *The Tyranny of Time* that our first challenge is simply finding time to get together. He writes:

> It is not enough to grab a few minutes here or there....Quality can be present in even minimal periods of time together. But over the long term, there is no quality without quantity.[2]

Professor Banks wonders if there couldn't be some formula to help us figure out how much quantity time we must spend to achieve quality. For example, if we spend an hour with our children at the park, does that guarantee us at least fifteen minutes of "quality time"?

Unfortunately, there is no such guarantee and there is no formula. Quality time is unpredictable, often a serendipity, a pleasant surprise that just "seems to happen."

Let's take one more look at Ephesians 5:15-17 (also discussed in chapter 22):

> See then that you walk circumspectly, not as fools but as wise, redeeming the time, because the

days are evil. Therefore do not be unwise, but understand what the will of the Lord is. (*NKJV*)

If you've ever been to a Christian time management seminar or read a Christian time management book or article, you have probably noticed that this verse is often quoted in the context of making the best possible use of

---

Take advantage of opportunities for quality moments when they present themselves within the larger quantities of time that you schedule with clocks, calendars and appointment books.

---

every minute, being efficient in scheduling, not wasting a second—in short, "getting more organized."

While getting organized is a good idea, it isn't the main thrust of this passage. In Ephesians 5:15, the word "time" means "opportunity" and the word "redeem" means "buy up." The Weymouth translation puts it best concerning time when it says, "Buy up your opportunities." Take advantage of opportunities for quality moments when they present themselves within the larger quantities of time that you schedule with clocks, calendars and appointment books.

There is no magic formula for this. Usually it takes hard work, combined with an awareness of just when opportunities might be available. Above all, it often involves a basic shift in attitude, particularly if you lean toward being a workaholic to any degree. Hugh, the semi-workaholic mentioned in chapter 16, was spending long hours at the office, coupled with frequent trips out of town. The bottom line: he just wasn't around that much.

Ironically, however, Hugh had the impression that, because he had no bad habits like watching football on TV all weekend, hanging out in bars, playing poker with friends or rebuilding engines in his garage with a bottle of beer handy, what time he was with his wife and three sons somehow added up to "quality." He may never have discovered otherwise if life hadn't dealt him a blow that eventually got his attention.

During a period of upheaval at his company, which involved many personnel changes, Hugh became unemployed. After he had drawn his last paycheck with the company to which he had given ten years of faithful service, Hugh sat down with his wife, Lenore, to talk about their future, which looked bleak. He never forgot what she told him:

"Hugh, I know you won't be able to understand this, but I've never felt more secure and more loved than right now, with you unemployed and us having no idea of how we're going to pay the mortgage, what we're going to do next or where we're going to go."

Dumbfounded, Hugh asked Lenore exactly why she felt this way and her answer came as a total shock. For the first time, she told him, she felt that he really needed her and that he was not a self-contained robot who simply went to work and came home when he got ready. Now at last they had a connection, they were actually going through something together.

Hugh realized for the first time that he had been so

dependent on his job and the loyalty of his employer that he had put his family much too low on his priority list. He was actually surprised to learn that there were no "company policies" he had to live up to at home in order to be accepted and loved. He had thought his employer had loved him unconditionally, but his naiveté had been shattered. Now he realized that his wife and sons were really the ones who loved him unconditionally, and that his first priorities should lie with them.

For the next two months, Hugh made a conscious effort to reconnect with his wife and sons after years of virtually ignoring them. He also went about trying to find a new job as he learned what it was like to be unemployed. The first real sting came the day he had to go to the local agency and collect his first unemployment check.

As he stood in line with a group of mostly day laborers, he kept thinking, "I don't belong here," and then he felt guilty for being a snob. Several weeks and four unemployment checks later, Hugh got an interview at an excellent firm and was offered a new position that paid better than his previous one.

Hugh's new job was also more demanding and he actually had more work to do, but instead of having time to wander from office to office and "talk business" during long lunches and coffee breaks, Hugh buckled down every second in order to be on his way home by 5:00. Slowly, he, Lenore and the boys turned the corner.

Hugh didn't do anything spectacular, but he did try to be more aware and more focused when he came through the door each evening. Instead of flopping on the couch with the paper and grunting that he wanted to be left alone, he stopped to talk with Lenore, or he would check with the boys on their homework, or play a little catch with them in the back yard. On weekends, he fought to find some time to take his sons out, one-on-one, for a hamburger or a Coke.

When Lenore told him that one thing she didn't like was his "lack of spontaneity," he started taking her out on simple little dates, like a cup of coffee, while the boys stayed with their grandmother who lived just a few blocks away.

Naturally, Hugh had to fight temptations to go back to the old patterns. Sometimes, in fact, he did have to work longer hours just to cover a real work load, not one that he had accumulated by goofing off for part of the day. Nonetheless, Lenore and the boys were much happier and he felt much more involved with them.

Hugh fought to keep weekends from turning into nothing more than cutting the grass and other chores around the house on Saturday, followed by getting heavily involved in church services on Sunday. He made it a special point always to take the family out after church to eat at an economical restaurant or, on occasion, they went on picnics.

"I actually tried to put the apostle Paul's advice into action," Hugh told me over lunch. "I began buying up every opportunity I could to use time more effectively to communicate with Lenore and the boys."

One thing that really spurred Hugh on was seeing the James Dobson film series on the family at his church. It was the film on Christian fathers that really got him. Dr. Dobson pointed out that men, in particular, are often all tied up in their careers and achievements, but ultimately every man would some day lie on his death bed and be surrounded by his family, particularly his children. And what would these children remember as they held their father's hand and tried to comfort him in his final hours?

Would they see someone who had always been a

stranger to them—always on the run, always looking forward to Mondays, even on Friday? Or would they see a man who had taken time to play catch and to wrestle on the rug? Would they see someone who realized that some kind of phony attempt to pass off a few minutes as "quality time" wouldn't make it—that quantity time was required and in the final analysis, quantity time is quality time?

"Dr. Dobson asked every man in the audience to think about how he was investing his life," Hugh recalled. "Was I investing it in my relationship to God, my wife, and my children, who would someday produce grandchildren—a posterity that would outlast my own frail lifetime? That's a question I keep asking myself every day, because the struggle isn't over."

We'll look at more of Hugh's story in chapter 26. Already, however, he has demonstrated that, regardless of what he does for a living, a father already has a major job—living with and leading his family. Every day Dad faces choices. He can be selfish, inconsiderate, preoccupied, or "just too busy with all this work down here at the office" to spend much time with his wife and/or children. Or he can build quality into their lives—and his.

Lord, they're going to be like me; therefore,
I want to be like You.

Analyze your relationships with your spouse and children. Do a little inventory on how you spend your time daily. Actually try keeping a log over the period of a week from when you get up in the morning to when you go to bed at night. How much "quantity time" do you actually get with your spouse and kids? How much time do you really plan for and how much "just happens"? Of the quantities of time you spend—great or small—how many moments would you rate as "quality" time? What steps could you take to increase the possibilities for "quality time" with your family?

Notes
1. Dennis Rainey, *Lonely Husbands, Lonely Wives* (Dallas: WORD Publishing, 1989), p. 190.
2. Robert Banks, *The Tyranny of Time* (Downers Grove: InterVarsity Press, 1983), p. 232.

CHAPTER TWENTY-SIX

Lord, Please Take This Job and Bless It

"One minute to five is the moment of triumph. You physically turn off the machine that has dictated to you all day long."

—A factory worker[1]

"When God gives any man wealth and possessions, and enables him to enjoy them, to accept his lot and be happy in his work—this is a gift of God."

—Ecclesiastes 5:19

Why are you working?

Since you will spend a huge part of your life at it—some say the average person puts in 100,000 hours over a fifty-year work span—it's a good question.[2] Most people claim they prefer work that is meaningful and enjoyable, but millions of them appear to live a different reality. Their theme song is, "I owe, I owe, it's off to work I go," and their credo, the infamous T.G.I.F. No matter what they do the rest of the week, they always thank God on Friday.

One study revealed that up to 80 percent of working Americans had jobs that did not make use of their talents. Another consulting firm estimates that only one-third of the people they study for management positions are really well suited for their jobs. Conservatively, 50 percent of all working Americans probably shouldn't be in their present jobs.[3]

These statistics are pretty ominous for anyone, but if we toss in a Christian value system we must also ask:

> Is what I'm doing worthwhile, as far as the Kingdom is concerned?
> Is my career God's will for my life?

The first question is easier to answer than the second. Despite all the bad press given the Puritan work ethic, which has been blamed for everything from the alcoholic syndrome to the cult of the self-made person, the Puritans had a much more God-centered attitude toward work than they are given credit for. In truth, the Puritans gave dignity to life's labors but never encouraged godless greed and materialism.

Puritans, by the way, got many of their ideas from the Reformers, not the least of whom was Martin Luther who proclaimed that clergymen, monks and nuns weren't doing work that was any holier than that of housewives and shopkeepers. In his commentary on Genesis, Luther wrote: "Household tasks have 'no appearance of sanctity' and yet these very works in connection with the household are more desirable than all the works of all the monks and nuns."[4]

Following in Luther's footsteps, the Puritan scholar, William Tyndale, added, "There is a difference betwixt washing of dishes and preaching of the Word of God; but as touches to please God, none at all."[5]

Okay, if spiritual heavyweights like Martin Luther and William Tyndale believed all honorable work has intrinsic value that glorifies God, what about being sure that your work is God's will for your life? Some people just seem to know that they are in the right job. It's as if God personally talks with them each morning, saying, "This is where I want you—you're doing a terrific job! Keep it up!"

Many others, however, struggle with career choices. If you doubt this, talk to any high school counselor. Fortunately, there are all kinds of good help available, some of which is written specifically for Christians.[6]

Even though you may use intelligence and common sense to find a job, it doesn't always work out. What if you think you have a direct call from God and then one day you get a direct call from a vice-president who doesn't seem to have gotten the same divine information? That was precisely the dilemma faced by Hugh, our pseudo workaholic friend introduced in chapters 16 and 25. He had worked faithfully for the same firm for ten years and had risen to sales manager. Suddenly, he was offered a new opportunity to become a sales representative in a distant state with very few trees and many prairie dog holes. It was that or move on, and Hugh chose to move on.

It was a devastating change. Hugh's "total commitment" and love for his company had gone unrequited. He had given his all and gotten the gate. But after the initial shock wore off, Hugh set about finding a new job with his usual efficient thoroughness. Over the next few weeks, he put out at least seventy-five resumés and cover letters to organizations all over the United States. With his three-piece suit carefully pressed, he was ready for interviews at the drop of a phone call.

A few nibbles came through, but none of them seemed particularly interesting. Then he got a call from a large Christian organization in his immediate area. A hurried and hassled vice president was on the line. Had he seen Hugh's meticulously prepared resumé and cover letter? Not exactly. Among his first words were, "Hugh, I have your name here on a slip of paper. Can you tell me why I'm calling you?"

Undismayed, Hugh seized the opportunity to tell the confused vice president a little bit about himself. He was just getting warmed up when the vice president interrupted, "Sounds good! Why don't you come down for an interview? You sound like a candidate for one of our vice president positions!"

A few days later, Hugh was in the executive's office and chatted for an hour about a vice presidential level job in company operations. But as good as it sounded, he decided not to take it.

"I could set this new department up for you," he explained to the amazed executive, "but I really wouldn't be interested in keeping it going. It's just not my thing."

Sure that he was back on the street to continue looking for work, Hugh got up to leave, but his interviewer called him back, saying, "Just a minute. I think we might have something else...."

After forty more minutes of conversation, Hugh finally

left. Three weeks later he was offered a job at a new level in the company where he had interviewed. "It was higher than a manager, but lower than a vice president," he recalls. "But it was a dream job for me, letting me use my marketing training in a management role."

"Your story has the proverbial happy ending," I told Hugh. "What are some principles you've gained from your experience that you could share with others—whether or not they may be as fortunate as you were."

"One thing I've learned was that at my former job my whole ego was tied up in who I was and what I was going to be and do when I got my next big promotion. I was playing around the edges of being a workaholic and spending more time down at the office than I did with my family. I believe God had to grab me by the scruff of the neck and let me know my priorities were fouled up. You could even say my job was my idol, but when all that got taken away I could see clearly for the first time, and in my new position God restored all of it ten-fold."

Hugh stayed in his "dream job" for the next five years, always struggling with keeping his priorities straight because he loved what he was doing and was often tempted to start working overtime for the sheer pleasure of it. But then he remembered his commitment to Lenore and the boys. Whenever he had the option, which was often, he left work at 5:00 to meet his goal of spending enough quantity time to find those precious moments of quality time that would make a real difference in all of their lives (see chapter 25).

Recently, Hugh moved on to a third job, which has given him more responsibility and even better rewards. Not only are the salary and benefits excellent, but he feels more fulfilled in being a good steward of his God-given talents and abilities.

While interviewing for his latest position, Hugh told his prospective employer, "One thing I've learned is exactly who I am. I've learned that I don't need a job to be a man, and I won't prove my manhood by pouring endless hours into something that can cause me to neglect my family."

That sounded good to the new employer, but Hugh had one other problem to iron out before coming on board. Despite the strides he had made to cure his workaholic tendencies, Hugh's natural drive and ambition had drawn him into taking more and more responsibilities. During the past five years he had been fairly happy with his "dream job," but he realized parts of it had been pulling him away from what he really loved to do. He had felt, however, it would have shown weakness to say something like, "May I be relieved of some of these jobs so I can do what I have a passion for?" He had been afraid that his employers would have countered, "You mean, you can't handle this? You just want a little job? Maybe we're paying you too much. We'll have to think about that when you're up for your next promotion."

The major reason Hugh had considered an offer from the new firm was that he realized that true success lay in zeroing in on your passion, if at all possible. As he talked with his new employer, he was able to structure a job where he could focus on what he really loved to do: working with smaller numbers of people to help them be as creative and productive as possible.

"My bottom line advice," Hugh said, "is that anyone who's not totally happy with his career should quit trying to be all things to all people—quit trying to juggle a quantity of duties. Ask yourself, 'What do I really want to do? What do I love to do?' Then do it!"

It's important to add that, for Hugh, "doing what you love" is not the same as "doing what you please." For the

Christian, underlying any search for a career or profession must be a deep desire to "glorify God and enjoy Him (not the job) forever." Without that primary goal, any "search for fulfillment" will be doomed to empty disappointment. Hugh agrees that it would help to modify the advice to "Do what you love" to say, "Do what you love for the One you love and the ones He gave you to love."

For the Christian, underlying any search for a career or profession must be a deep desire to "glorify God and enjoy Him (not the job) forever."

When considering any job, it's perfectly natural to ask, "How much does it pay? What are the benefits? Is it 'upwardly mobile'?" None of those questions, however, was asked by the men Christ called to be His disciples. On the Damascus road, Paul didn't want to know about perks, he only wanted to know, "What will You have me to do?"[7]

If the statistics quoted earlier in this chapter are anywhere close to correct, many Christians are staying in rat race type jobs where they don't belong due to inertia, fear or quiet desperation. Work done to please God, however, can take you beyond the rat race where you will find that the preacher's words from Ecclesiastes are true: You can do nothing better than eat, drink, and find satisfaction in your work,[8] because it is done to please Him.

Lord, why am I working? I know you designed me for a

certain task. If You can't bless what I'm doing, help me understand why.

You may not always be able to do "exactly what you love," but you can always do what you do out of love and integrity. The following "pledge" is a partial paraphrase of Romans 12:9-21:

I won't be hypocritical but will love my fellow workers.

My dislike of evil will be evidenced by my desire for what is good and pure.

I'll be a fervent, diligent worker, and will realize that my behavior at work reflects on my Lord. My good, hard work is probably a more important testimony than a lot of talk.

I'll rejoice in hope, persevere through rough days.

I'll devote myself to prayer about my job, my fellow employees and my boss.

When I'm mistreated at work I'll keep my mouth shut unless I can say something constructive.

I'll be known for self-respect and respect for others...not for revenge.

My constant desire at work will be to live for the Lord. I want to overcome evil with good, and never be overcome by evil.[9]

Notes
1. This remark was made by one of 133 workers interviewed by Studs Terkel, *Working: People Talk About What They Do All Day and How They Feel About What They Do* (New York: Pantheon, 1972).

2. See Ted W. Engstrom and R. Alec Mackenzie, *Managing Your Time* (Grand Rapids: Zondervan Books, 1967), p. 19.
3. Interview of Arthur F. Miller, Jr., and Ralph Mattson, "Find Your Niche," *Eternity*, November 1982, pp. 21,22. Miller and Mattson direct People Management, Inc., a consulting firm used by corporations and organizations to analyze gifts and "patterns" of abilities. They are co-authors of *Finding a Job You Can Love* published by Thomas Nelson, 1982.
4. Luther makes this observation on his commentary on Genesis 13:13, quoted by Leland Ryken, "Puritan Work Ethic: The Dignity of Life's Labors," *Christianity Today*, October 19, 1979, p. 15.
5. From Tyndale's book, *Parable of the Wicked Mammon*, quoted by Leland Ryken, "The Puritan Work Ethic: The Dignity of Life's Labors," Christianity Today, October 19, 1979, p. 15.
6. See especially *Christian Career Planning*, John Bradley (available through Interchristo, P.O. Box 33487, Seattle, WA, 98133, Phone: 800-426-1342); *Life Planning*, Farnsworth and Lawhead (InterVarsity Press); *What Color Is Your Parachute?* Richard Bolles (Ten Speed Press); and *The Truth About You*, Miller and Mattson (Fleming H. Revell Company).
7. See Paul's account of his conversion as told to the hostile crowd in Acts 21 and 22. See especially Acts 22:10.
8. See Ecclesiastes 2:24.
9. Dick Staub, "9 to 5: A New Look at Christian Career Choices," *Eternity*, October 1981, p. D9.

CHAPTER TWENTY-SEVEN

Can Anyone Really "Have It All"?

"If having it all means doing it all, can't I have just a little less?"

—A working mom[1]

"Charm is deceptive, and beauty is fleeting; but a woman who fears the Lord is to be praised."

—Proverbs 31:30

Sally's day begins at 5:30 A.M. when she and husband, Brad, roll out of bed. Sally gets their three small children up and proceeds to get them dressed while somehow getting herself ready for work, as well. She is glad that Brad can dress himself, although he usually needs help finding clean socks or choosing a tie. Brad is color blind, and unless Sally checks him out before they leave for work, he is always in danger of looking like a rainbow that collided with a comet.

After breakfast, hurriedly prepared by Sally, they all fly out of the house, pile into their van and roar off to day care, kindergarten, second grade and jobs. Fortunately, commuting to work is simplified because Sally and Brad work for the same corporation, Sally as a designer and Brad as an engineer.

That afternoon, Sally and Brad leave work promptly at 5:00, pick up Billy at day care and head on home. Jimmy, their kindergartner, and Sarah, their second grader, are already there, in the care of Sally's mother, who lives nearby and takes care of the children each afternoon when they get home from school.

"Thanks, Mom," Sally tells her mother as she leaves. "Without you, we'd be sunk."

But Sally's day is a long way from over.

Banishing Sarah to her room to finish up some spelling homework, Sally does her best to get through "piranha hour" as Jimmy and Billy pester her for snacks, drinks and attention. Finally, she can take it no longer and calls Brad in from the living room where he's been looking through the mail and glancing at the 6:00 o'clock news.

"Brad, I've got to get dinner and the boys are being pests—can you take them for a while?"

"Sure, Honey," Brad says cheerfully, and off he and the boys go for a pre-dinner wrestling match.

Bless his heart, Sally muses. He's not too perceptive about what needs to be done but he's always willing to help when I ask him. Later, dinner finished, Brad cleans up the kitchen while Sally bathes Billy and gets him into bed. Then it's Jimmy's turn, and later, Sarah's. Being older, Sarah gets to stay up to watch "The Cosby Show," but finally they're all in bed and it's time to relax, right?

Not quite. Sally has to iron outfits for herself and the three children for the next day, as well as one of Brad's shirts. Then, after folding several loads of clothes and doing some other routine chores, she falls into bed at 11:15.

Brad has also come to bed, after going over some reports he needs to discuss in a meeting the next day. As they lie in the darkness, they try to talk for a few minutes—"communicate meaningfully" is how their Bible teacher put it in class last Sunday.

"Sally, I've been thinking," Brad says after they discuss Sarah's reading problems, which her teacher has called to their attention. "What do you say we get a sitter Friday night and go out for a quick bite and maybe a movie....Sally? Sally, are you asleep?"

Sally is, indeed, asleep. Another day is done—and so is she.

At times Sally asks herself the question that opened the last chapter: "Why are you working?" She isn't a single mom with kids to support, so that isn't it. Brad's salary as an engineer is adequate, but Sally's salary makes it possible to get a lot of things they would have to do without, chiefly their first home, which they just purchased after years of living in apartments. So, that's partly it.

But if Sally is honest, the biggest reason she works is that she enjoys her job. It makes her feel as if she has worth and importance. She enjoys the meetings, the deadlines and the challenges of the fast-paced corporate world. As much as she loves her kids, she is glad her days consist of more than vacuuming up Cheerios, unplugging toilets and wiping noses.

When she and Brad set a goal to buy the new house, she gladly accepted the double burden of being Mom and breadwinner. Brad has been a gem in many ways, but much of the load of keeping the home going continues to fall on Sally.

Sally, of course, realizes she is no longer the exception but the rule. If anyone has "come a long way, Baby" it is the working woman. Consider a few statistics:

- As the 1960s began, 34.8 percent of women were in the work force. As the 1980s came to a close, the figure was closer to 60 percent and climbing.[2]
- In 1970, one percent of all business travelers were women. By 1985, 30 percent of business travelers were women, running up their frequent flyer benefits to the tune of twenty-three billion dollars annually.
- In 1972, seventy thousand women held American Express cards. By 1984, that number had risen to 4.5 million.
- By the year 2000, it is estimated that 50 percent of all business travelers will be women.[3]

Diane Von Furstenberg, whose fashion empire includes eye wear, makeup, home furnishings and luggage, spends three hundred hours a year in the air. She says: "Women today have to be organized. You have to work at your business, at the way you look, at your family, your relationships. The more you have, the more it takes to make everything work."[4]

In their insightful book *The Curious Waltz of the Work-*

You can search the parables, Beatitudes, conversations, debates and discourses of Jesus and you will find no instructions on "how to have it all."

---

ing Woman, Karen Scalf Linamen and Linda Holland agree that being organized is important, but to find true success as a working woman you need to delve deeper. They believe that "success begins, instead, with matters of the heart and mind. Before we can talk about ways to improve what we do, we need to take a good look at who we are."[5]

Both women speak from personal experience. A single mother for eleven years, Linda has reared two sons and a daughter. The boys, now in junior and senior high school, both live at home. Her daughter, now in her 20s, is married.

Karen is a full time free-lance writer who works out of her home while mothering preschool-age Kaitlyn. Before she chose full time free-lance work in order to have more time to spend with Kaitlyn, Karen had been a staff editor for a large Christian organization, as well as a producer of a daily television talk show.

In their book, the authors come to grips with the "schizophrenic dilemma" all working mothers face. The patient, sensitive, nurturing mother at home must switch gears when she heads for the office, where she is expected to be aggressive, tough and someone who gets results. At the end of the day, she must switch gears and go back where she is expected to be her other sweet self. As Linda and Karen put it, "The office demands a tiger, but husbands prefer a lamb. The kids need a hybrid of disciplinarian, playmate and friend. The church wants a servant."[6]

The end result for almost every woman is stress, tension, fatigue—and guilt. If she's lucky, her husband will offer to help. More and more men are overcoming the centuries of "macho training" that told them a man is supposed to be the tough, strong breadwinner, while the home is the domain of the wife. In recent years, macho men are out and sensitive, caring husbands are in, but it's still slow going. And, even with the change in husband attitudes, there is little doubt that women remain the heart of a home.

One sociologist who studied fifty-two career couples learned that the working wife usually comes home to a "second shift" and does 75 percent of the household tasks.[7] Another research firm reports that when husbands do housework, they usually take the jobs already assigned to the children in the family. Wives still wind up doing anywhere from two-thirds to 80 percent of shopping, laundry, cooking, cleaning, child care and paperwork.[8]

So the woman who seeks to "have it all"—which generally means being a wife, mother and having a successful career, as well—faces a big Catch 22. Can she have it all and do it all, as well?

Despite the impression being given by chic upwardly mobile guests on talk shows, the answer is no.

With only twenty-four hours in a day, we all have to make choices. Having it all really isn't one of them. As Linamen and Holland say, "Nobody can have it all. Nobody can do it all. Not women. Not men. And most importantly, not all at the same time."[9]

Whenever you try to have it all, something or someone has to suffer. According to a telephone poll of one thousand adult women, 12 percent believed career suffered most, 28 percent named marriage, and 42 percent admitted that children suffered most of all.[10]

Something else that can suffer is your core relationship with God. To ask, "Why can't I have it all?" deftly leaves God out of the picture or relegates Him to being "The Big Career Booster in the Sky" who is supposed to send energy, patience, and self-control, mixed with love, joy, peace and longsuffering. And don't forget an occasional bit of divine intervention to boost the climb up the career ladder.

You can search the parables, Beatitudes, conversations, debates and discourses of Jesus and you will find no instructions on "how to have it all." He does mention seeking first the kingdom of God and not worrying about basic needs because they will be taken care of, but He never encourages the juggling of so many responsibilities, so many possessions and so many ambitions that you are left distracted, tired and frustrated—barely able to go through the spiritual motions.

And yet the temptation to try to do it all is still there, especially for the working mother. She will turn all those stones into bread if it kills her. Perhaps she has juggled schedules so she can have the children covered with day care, a neighbor or, like Sally, a grandparent.

Perhaps she has her husband trained (at least partly) to help at home and he's getting better.

Perhaps she has come to grips with what she can do or not do and is learning how to say no.

Perhaps she has even perfected the art of "selective cleaning" and she can let certain things go without guilt pangs.

She may even have worked out traveling the perils of the "mommy track," that much publicized "secondary status" given to mothers who decide they cannot give their all to the company because they must be available to their families at home.

Or she may be "sequencing" for a few years—staying home with the kids until they can function better on their own, but planning to return to work, well aware that she has lost some irreplaceable time that could affect her career.

There is a myriad of bases to cover for wives and mothers who are carving out a career in the marketplace. The danger is they can touch all the bases but feel that something is still missing. To paraphrase W. B. Yeats' well-known poem, "Things fall apart when the center isn't there."

What exactly is the center? Henri Nouwen puts it this way:

> Jesus calls it the Kingdom, the Kingdom of His Father. For us in the twentieth century, this may not have much meaning. Kings and kingdoms do not play an important role in our daily life. But only when we understand Jesus' words as an urgent call to make the life of God's Spirit our priority can

we see better what is at stake. A heart set on the Father's Kingdom is also a heart set on the spiritual life. To set our hearts on the Kingdom, therefore, means to make the life of the Spirit within and among us, the center of all we think, say or do.[11]

Seek first the center. Never let it go. Then all the others things will fall—by the wayside or into their proper place.

Lord, I know "having it all" is a trap;
I prefer to want all of You.

Reread Henri Nouwen's words near the end of this chapter and analyze your own schedule. Are you dealing with the pressures and tensions of life from the center—the life of the Spirit within you—or are you desperately trying to cope with all of the peripheral, urgent things that must be done and letting the center go because there just doesn't seem to be enough time?

Notes
1. Karen Scalf Linamen and Linda Holland, *The Curious Waltz of the Working Woman* (Ventura: Regal Books, 1990).
2. See Claudia Wallis, "Onward, Women!" *Time,* December 4, 1989, p. 82.
3. Dena Kaye, "Jet Propelled Women," *United,* April 1985, p. 41.
4. See Dena Kaye, "Jet Propelled Women," *United,* April 1985, p. 49.
5. Karen Scalf Linamen and Linda Holland, *The Curious Waltz of the Working Woman.*
6. Ibid.
7. See Claudia Wallis, p. 86, who refers to Arlie Hochschild's book, *The Second Shift* (1989). Hochschild believes that men are "trying to have their wives' salaries and still have the traditional roles at home."
8. Reported in *Bottom Line/Personal,* February 15, 1990, p. 9. These findings are by researchers Linda Waite and Frances Goldscheider, The Rand Corporation, a research firm in Santa Monica, California.

9. Karen Scalf Linamen and Linda Holland, *The Curious Waltz of the Working Woman.*

10. This poll was conducted for *Time* magazine in the fall of 1989 by Yankelovich Clancy Shulman. Statistics quoted in Claudia Wallis, "Onward, Women!" *Time*, December 4, 1989, p. 86.

11. Henri J. M. Nouwen, *Making All Things New* (San Francisco: Harper and Row Publishers, 1981), p. 43.

CHAPTER TWENTY-EIGHT

Seize Your Time or Lose the Day

Gather ye rosebuds
while ye may,
Old Time is still a-flying,
And this same flower that
smiles today
Tomorrow will be a-dying.
—Robert Herrick (1591-1674)

"But I pray to you, O Lord, in the
time of your favor."
—Psalm 69:13

In 1989, a film with the unlikely title, *Dead Poets' Society,* made a brief bid for top box office receipts.1 Its star was also unlikely—at least for me. The name Robin Williams conjures up thoughts of "Mork and Mindy," not a teacher of literature at an exclusive boys' prep school in New England. Nonetheless, Williams was perfect for the part, mixing erudition with humor and passion to turn on his students to a different kind of drug—the sheer excitement of the imagery and truth contained in classic poetry.

How did Williams do it? He started on his first day of class when he invited everyone out in the hall to gaze with him at trophy cases containing photos of young men who had won school honors in years gone by. His brief but eloquent pep talk featured one brief Latin phrase—*carpe diem*—"Seize the day." Williams told his students that every one of them had the same opportunity to gain honor and glory—not necessarily by winning some trophy—but in the sheer joy of learning and becoming more than they had ever been before.

Standing behind his class as they gazed at the trophies and photos, Williams had them imagine they could hear the whispered voices of those from the past urging everyone there to "seize the day." As his hoarse stage whisper of "CARPE DIEM" pounded on the doors of their minds, you could see the lights go on.

That scene set the course for the entire film, which is a heartwarming story of how a literature teacher breaks all protocol in a stuffy, confining, unimaginative setting to fire the imaginations of his students to go beyond themselves—to do and be more than they had ever dreamed of. Their time was now—but they had to reach out to make it happen. They had to seize the day.

Although Robin Williams used the phrase carpe diem a bit inaccurately in order to reach a noble goal,[2] he did point toward a principle that Scripture teaches in several places. "Making hay while the sun shines" isn't the precise idea, but it comes close. In the New Testament, Paul says it best when he quotes the prophet Isaiah to the Corinthians: "In the time of my favor I will answer you, and in the day of salvation I will help you," and then Paul goes on to say, "I tell you, now is the time of God's favor, now is the day of salvation" (see Isa. 49:8; 2 Cor. 6:2).

You can find this same idea in the Psalms, for example: "But I pray to you, O Lord, in the time of your favor; in your great love, O God, answer me with your sure salvation" (Ps. 69:13).

Passages like these make it clear that the Christian is in a unique position—able to call upon the favor and love of God. What better reason to seize the day—especially the hours and minutes that make up that day.

Setting goals, deciding on priorities and making plans is a great strategy (see chapters 22 through 24), but like any strategy it requires the spark that will fire us into action. Whatever you do about the time crunch, there has to be a moment when you say, "carpe diem." If you don't seize the time in your day, someone else will, as Gordon MacDonald explains in *Ordering Your Private World*. "MacDonald's Laws of Unseized Time" include:

Law 1: Unseized Time Flows Toward My Weaknesses
Law 2: Unseized Time Comes Under the Influence of Dominant People in My World
Law 3: Unseized Time Surrenders to the Demands of All Emergencies
Law 4: Unseized Time Gets Invested in Things That Gain Public Acclamation[3]

MacDonald's first law about unseized time flowing

toward one's weaknesses poses the question: "Are you spending your time at what you're good at, or on other tasks that perhaps other people could do?" That's an excellent question for a busy executive—in fact, it's a good question for anyone, even working women with families.

Mothers who are holding down full-time jobs outside the home may laugh hysterically at the concept of "unseized time." All their time was seized long ago and, besides, to whom would they delegate all those jobs that only they can do?

Perhaps that's just the point. Society lets most moms know in blatant or sometimes subtle ways that they are the ones who "do it all." And so, believing all their press clippings, they dutifully jump through a lot of hoops of their own making.

Perhaps it's time for Mom to reconsider. Does she really have to do it all? What about her husband and her children? Perhaps some gentle but firm confrontations would yield some positive results. Some husbands are more willing to help than their wives may think. Depending on their age, children can be trained to do simple tasks like picking up their toys or perhaps more difficult chores like making beds or even making lunches.

And if there is no one in your family to whom you can turn for help, there are always outside sources who can be hired. That may take a bite out of the family income, but it's better than being consumed by trying to do it all.

MacDonald's second law about unseized time getting snatched away by dominant people is all too true. There is always someone who has a wonderful plan for your life, and they will spend much of your life telling you about it if you don't seize your time. Who are the dominant, assertive, aggressive, squeaky-wheel people in your world?

Unless you take positive action on your own behalf, they will always move in to influence and consume your unseized time.

MacDonald's third law is another way of saying that the tyranny of the urgent will always consume your day unless you find ways to fight back. There should, however, be ways to sort out some of life and not leave it all at

---

The tyranny of the urgent always threatens the sanctity of the important.

---

the mercy of "emergencies." As Gordon MacDonald observes, "Not everything that cries the loudest is the most urgent thing."[4]

MacDonald's fourth law seems keyed more to pastors and other visible types who have to be up in front. For many others, however, there is something magnetic about invitations from people who "just know that you're the perfect one for this job." This often happens at church, where, unfortunately, there may be no one else who wants to do it at the moment. But it can happen in other settings, as well. The trap always lies in "What will people think if I don't accept their invitation?" If you haven't seized your time, you probably won't have a good reason to refuse and you will be snared again.

So what does it mean to "seize one's time"? How is unseized time recaptured and used effectively? One of Gordon MacDonald's best suggestions is to seize your time by budgeting it far in advance because, "Here's where the battle is won or lost."[5] MacDonald's own approach is to enter the principle elements of his time budget into his calendar eight weeks in advance of when they will happen. He writes:

> And what goes into the calendar? Those non-negotiable aspects of my private world: my spiritual disciplines, my mental disciplines, my Sabbath rest and, of course, my commitments to family and special friendships. Then a second tier of priorities will enter the calendar: schedule of the main work to which I am committed—sermon study, writing, leadership development, and discipling.[6]

The key phrase MacDonald uses is "nonnegotiable aspects of my private world." He seizes his time simply by scheduling time he wants to be nonnegotiable, time that he knows is so important he will not give it up, not even for the urgent demands that clamor to be heard. And he finds that if he enters his nonnegotiables into his calendar eight weeks ahead, as the time approaches for those non-negotiables to happen, other demands do hammer at him from all sides.

Some urgent requests are legitimate, of course, and he has to be flexible; many, however, are not. Many can wait or not be done at all. He can turn these requests down, knowing that he has already scheduled an evening with his wife or his children, or a special hour of study and prayer.

As MacDonald puts it, "How much better my private world is when I allow that work to flow around the priorities and into the available slots than when things are the other way around."

If you are thinking, "This chapter is a reminder of the importance of priorities," you are right. The tyranny of the urgent always threatens the sanctity of the important. Mac-Donald continually found that the important, nonnegotiable times he penciled in his calendar eight weeks ahead all had something in common—they could be neglected and there would be no repercussions, at least at first.

If he missed a quiet time with God, it would be okay; after all, God is gracious. If he missed time with his family, Gail and the children would understand and forgive. If he missed some study hours he had set aside because he knew he needed to prepare for a future sermon series, no one would necessarily be the wiser—until he preached that series and he (and possibly others) realized he hadn't done as good a job as he could have.

Unfortunately, the important things can be ignored and neglected without immediate consequences. But it's also true that what goes around comes around and when neglect of the important finally surfaces there is usually a heavy price to pay.

Perhaps Gordon MacDonald's theories, written from his pastor's study, seem a bit ivory tower and far removed from your workaday world. You may not have as much control as he does over what you can put into your calendar and call "nonnegotiable." But he has decided upon one nonnegotiable that everyone, from busy mother to harried executive (who sometimes may be the same person) can choose. MacDonald illustrates that essential element by telling of the time a man asked him if they could have an early morning breakfast together. Because he knew MacDonald was an early riser, he suggested 6:00 A.M.

MacDonald looked at his calendar and said he already had an appointment for that hour, but would the man be willing to do it at 7:00? The man agreed, but looked surprised that someone's calendar might reflect plans for 6:00 in the morning. MacDonald writes:

I did have a commitment for 6:00 that morning,
in fact, it started earlier than that. It was a commitment to God. He was first on the calendar that day,
where He belongs every day. And it is not the sort
of commitment one compromises. Not if one
wants to seize time and keep it under control. It is
the start of an organized day, an organized life, and
an organized private world.[7]

Yes, the phone is ringing off the hook, the baby is cry-
ing, and your two-year-old is making a peanut butter
sandwich out of a hot pad. Yes, the report is due on Monday, the lawn looks like a hayfield ripe unto harvest.
Everyone and everything is clamoring for your attention.
But you still have a choice of who or what will seize
your precious hours and minutes.
"Now is the time of God's favor...." Carpe diem!

---

*Lord, give me energy, courage and foresight to
seize the day and use it well.*

List some things you may want to make nonnegotiable. For example.

- Quiet time to recharge my spiritual batteries.

- A weekly aerobic session at the gym.

- An afternoon out to shop or just do as I please.

- Regular dates with my spouse, son or daughter for
  one-on-one communication.

List your nonnegotiables. Then "SEIZE THE DAY!"

Notes

1. *Dead Poets' Society* finished ninth at $94.3 million, behind *Batman, Indiana Jones and the Last Crusade, Lethal Weapon 2, Honey, I Shrunk the Kids, Rain Man, Ghost Busters 2, Look Who's Talking,* and *Parenthood.*
2. See Eugene Ehrlich, Amo, Amas, Amat and More (New York: Harper and Row Publishers, 1985), p. 75. According to Latin scholar Ehrlich, carpe diem comes from "Odes," the work of the Latin poet, Horace (65-8 b.c.). The full thought of what Horace is trying to convey in the poem is to "enjoy today, trusting little in tomorrow." In other words, "Eat, drink and be merry, for tomorrow you may die," or, in the more colloquial terms, "Make hay while the sun shines because it's later than you think."
3. See Gordon MacDonald, *Ordering Your Private World* (Atlanta: Oliver Nelson, 1985), pp. 74-79.
4. Ibid., p. 78.
5. Ibid., p. 83.
6. Ibid., p. 84.
7. Ibid., p. 85.

CHAPTER TWENTY-NINE

A Time to Be Timely

Four things that never return:
The spoken word
The sped arrow,
The past life,
The neglected opportunity.

—Anonymous

"There is a right time for everything."

—Ecclesiastes 3:1 (*TLB*)

"EVERYBODY HAS THE SAME AMOUNT OF TIME!"

Time management books and articles often trumpet this astounding "fact" and, mathematically speaking, it is true. Every morning God doles out 86,400 seconds to every soul on the planet—1,440 minutes that add up to twenty-four hours for the day.

We can do what we want with this daily allotment: spend it, use it, waste it, kill it, invest it or just ignore it. But whatever we do with it, our time for one day will be gone. There is no way to save any of it. As someone said, "Life is like a coin: you can spend it any way you want to, but you can spend it only once."

The "seconds, minutes, hours approach" to time is what the Bible calls *chronos*. Whenever the Scripture writers refer to clock or calendar time, they use chronos, as in Matthew 2:7: "Then Herod called the Magi secretly and found out from them the exact time [chronos] the star had appeared." Chronos always refers to a space of time, whether short or long. And it is true, we all have the same amount of chronos in every twenty-four hour day.

But Scripture also speaks of another kind of time that is harder to pin down or calculate. Kairos means a certain period that is usually linked to some kind of event or opportunity. As Paul puts it in Galatians 6:10: "Therefore, as we have opportunity [kairos], let us do good to all people." Kairos also designates hope. Jesus began His public ministry by saying, "The time [kairos] has come. The kingdom of God is near" (see Mark 1:15).

As each of us deal with our 86,400 seconds each day, we have to think about both kinds of time. Chronos questions include: "How can I be efficient?" "How can I be sure I am on time?"

Kairos questions are: "How can I be effective? How can I seize the opportunities and be timely?"

One of the best descriptions of kairos time is found in Ecclesiastes 3:1-11. It was written by King Solomon, who spends most of the book of Ecclesiastes penning the confessions of a man who didn't always use his time as wisely as someone named King Solomon should. Yet, Solomon knew the right way, and in Ecclesiastes he gives us fourteen contrasts that make up a cross section of the ebb and flow of life.

> There is a time for everything, and a season for every activity under heaven: a time to be born and a time to die, a time to plant and a time to uproot, a time to kill and a time to heal, a time to tear down and a time to build, a time to weep and a time to laugh, a time to mourn and a time to dance, a time to scatter stones and a time to gather them, a time to embrace and a time to refrain, a time to search and a time to give up, a time to keep and a time to throw away, a time to tear and a time to mend, a time to be silent and a time to speak, a time to love and a time to hate, a time for war and a time for peace (Eccles. 3:1-8).

Many scholars believe Solomon wrote Ecclesiastes near the end of his life when, for him at least, everything was *déjà vu*. He had seen it all and decided most of it was meaningless. But in all the meaninglessness he also saw the symmetry and rhythm God had built into life. Life is a never-ending cycle and in these fourteen familiar contrasts we can find the events that most of us experience during our lives.

A random glance at these contrasts shows us that life is

full of opportunities—kairos times, which God has appointed and it is up to us to be aware, alert and ready to act. We don't think a lot about a *time to be born and a time to die* as we move through most of our lives. We're too busy growing up, getting an education, finding jobs, getting established, getting married, raising families, paying mortgages.

Sunrise and sunset come regularly and then one day—often it seems to happen in our forties—we realize we are on the downward side of life and it's getting a little steeper every year. Then we may start to think about "a time to die." And we wonder, "Did I accomplish enough? Did I accomplish *anything?*"

A time to plant and a time to uproot reminds us that there are times to start things and times to end things. There are times when bad habits have to go and new habits have to replace them. Debilitating relationships that drag us down must be severed and good relationships developed.

A time to tear down and a time to build makes us think of our "urban renewal projects," some of them very literal, like remodeling the kitchen. But lots of other things in life need tearing down and building up. We need to tear down walls that have risen between us and our mate, our children or our friends. We need to build bridges back to those who matter in our lives and we need to do all we can to build them up in the faith. In a very real sense, our lives are a testimony to what we have built and what we have torn down.

A time to tear and a time to mend suggests there are times when we need to tear some things up, tear other things away, and tear still other things apart. Tearing should be done carefully and be preceded by a great deal of thought and prayer. Mending is a loving word. It speaks of wanting to save something, wanting to make it work again and extend its usefulness. Who or what do you know that needs your mending touch?

A time to love and a time to hate seem to leave us in a dilemma. When are we supposed to hate? What or who is involved?

Scripture never teaches us to hate people, but it teaches

It is never too soon to be loving, but there are times when it could be too late.

---

us to hate injustice, dishonesty, prejudice and hypocrisy. We need to hate these things with perfect hatred and do all we can to stamp them out of our lives and out of our society where we can have an influence.

Any time we hate something, it should be because we love something else much more. Opportunities to love are all around us every day. We never know when a loving act can be timely, but a good rule of thumb is not to hold back with our love, but to share it generously, even recklessly, at times. It is never too soon to be loving, but there are times when it could be too late.

In one of his "Think It Over" columns, which appear in his church's weekly bulletin, Charles Swindoll shares the following story:

Last September, three years ago, Terry Shafer was strolling the shops in Moline, Illinois. She knew exactly what she wanted to get her husband for Christmas...but she realized it might be too expensive. A little shop on Fifth in Moline attracted Terry's attention, so she popped inside. Her eyes darted toward the corner display—"That's it!" she smiled as she nodded with pleasure. "How much?" she asked the shopkeeper, pointing in that direction.

"Only $127.50."

Her smile faded into disappointment as she realized David's salary couldn't stand such a jolt. He was feeding and clothing the family on a policeman's wage. It was out of the question. Yet she hated to give up without a try—so she applied a little womanly persistence.

"Uh, what about putting this aside for me? Maybe I could pay a little each week then pick it up a few days before Christmas?"

The merchant smiled as he studied her intensity. She *really* wanted it.

"No," he said, "I won't do that." But neither would he let her leave the store without it.

"I'll gift wrap it right now. You can take it with you and pay me later," he said to her surprise. Terry was elated. She agreed to pay so much every week, and she thanked and thanked the man as she left, explaining how delighted her husband would be.

"Oh, that's nothing at all," the shopkeeper answered, in no way realizing the significant role his generosity would play in the days ahead.

Then came Saturday, October 1.

Patrolman David Shafer, working the night shift, got a call in his squad car. A drugstore robbery was in progress. Officer Shafer reacted instantly. He arrived on the scene just in time to see the suspect speed away. With siren screaming and red lights flashing, he followed in hot pursuit. Three blocks later the getaway vehicle suddenly pulled over and stopped. The driver didn't move. Dave carefully approached the suspect with his weapon drawn. While only three feet from the driver's door, two things happened in a split second. The door flew open as the thief produced a .45-caliber pistol and fired at the policeman's abdomen.

At seven o'clock that morning another patrolman came to the door of Officer David Shafer's home. Wife Terry frowned as she cracked open the door. Calmly and with great care, the policeman explained what had happened in the early morning hours. Her husband had been courageous in pursuing a robbery suspect. There had been gunfire. David was hit. Shot at point-blank range.

Stunned, Terry thought how glad she was that she had not waited until Christmas to give her husband his present. How grateful she was that the shopkeeper had been willing to let her pay for it later.

Otherwise, Dave, struck with a devastatingly deadly .45-caliber slug in the stomach, would have surely died. Instead, he was now in the hospital—not with a gunshot wound, but with only a bad bruise.

You see, Christmas came early in 1977 for David Shafer of Moline, Illinois. He was wearing the gift of life Terry could not wait to give—his brand new bulletproof vest.[1]

There is much to be said for being "on time." *Chronos*—the pages of the calendar and the ticks of the clock—is an inescapable part of life. But *kairos*—the special moments to be timely—is even more important.

How's your timing been lately?

———

Lord, please improve my timing. I don't want to miss the opportunities you send my way.

———

Think of some kairos moments that have come your way lately. Use Ecclesiastes 3:1-8 to take inventory. Did you seize the opportunities to plant or uproot? What about tearing down and building up? What have you mended lately? What about biding your time or speaking up when it was needed? Above all, what opportunities to love have you seized and used? If your score could be better, don't be discouraged. Simply pray to be more aware of kairos—God's moments for the timely word or act.

Note
1. Charles Swindoll, "Think It Over," January 11, 1981, Fullerton Evangelical Free Church. Used by permission.

CHAPTER THIRTY

Letting Go to Let God In

Executives are hard to see
Their costly time I
may not waste;
I make appointments nervously
And talk to them in haste.
But any time of night or day,
In places suitable or odd,
I seek and get without delay
An interview with God.

—Anonymous

"Apart from me you can
do nothing."
—John 15:5

We are coming to the end of our thirty-part experiment, which was never intended as a collection of helpful hints on how to get control of your time and your life. Many excellent books can tell you how to do that.[1] Instead, these readings have emphasized *giving up control* and letting God run your particular show.

Perhaps this sounds like the well-known cliché, "Let go and let God," but I hope not. Letting go and letting God is too easily misconstrued by some to justify giving up and just drifting. Others claim they are letting go and letting God, but their lives are full of disorganized chaos or preoccupied busy-ness.

Preoccupation is one of our most common, but stress-filled, pastimes. As Henri Nouwen puts it, being preoccupied is filling your time and place long before you are there.[2] Instead of trusting God for today, we play the game of "what if?"

- What if I don't make the deadline?
- What if I get sick, or hurt or fired?
- What if Johnny doesn't learn to read better?
- What if the bill collectors won't leave us alone?

To play the game of "what if?" we learn certain negative skills—for example, *anticipation*. I try to anticipate what will happen, what people will do, even what God will do. That way I can strategize, plan and be ready to respond and react to what I think is going to happen. In this way I hope I can stay in control of what happens around me and to me.

Of course, this strategy doesn't always work. Some weeks it doesn't work at all! Life is full of the unexpected, well saturated with interruptions and other results of Murphy's Law: "Anything that can go wrong probably will."

In *Discovering the Depths*, William Clemmons points out that when we live life in the future, we miss out on the now:

> An overly anxious anticipation of all the events of one's life is a life lived for the most part in the future, unaware of the activity of God in the present moment. When we do that, we say that the future is in God's hands, *but* accomplished by our *power*. We attempt to make the future dependent on physical and intellectual power alone without a recognition of God's activity, protection and guidance.[3]

You try to play it safe but you are rushed and busy, trying to go it alone while God watches all your heroic efforts from the sidelines, waiting to be invited into the game.

Anticipating and controlling our time seem useful and at one level they are. But ultimate peace and fulfillment are not found in a Daytimer or executive organizer. You can be organized but still empty. You can make all your appointments on time and still feel as if you're late for something that you can't quite put your finger on.

You may tell yourself you have it all together, but a key part is still missing. Instead of wholeness, there is careful organization of a lot of fragments. You live under the tyranny of the urgent, efficiently taking care of all the ought's, should's and have-to's. You try to play it safe but you are rushed and busy, trying to go it alone while God watches all your heroic efforts from the sidelines, waiting to be invited into the game.

Wholeness, on the other hand, means you are "more relaxed, released, creative, risking, resourceful, slowed down, receptive and focused."[4] All those descriptions of wholeness sound familiar, like the Man who strides across the pages of Scripture with seven league boots bringing wholeness to a fragmented world. On practically every page of the Gospels, Jesus shows us how to be whole, but in a parable He told the night before He died He put it all in one simple phrase: "Abide in me!"

As Jesus and His disciples left the Upper Room, heading for the Mount of Olives, it appears that He stopped to call attention to a vine growing along the path:

> I am the true vine, and My Father is the vine-dresser. Every branch in Me that does not bear fruit He takes away; and every branch that bears fruit He prunes, that it may bear more fruit. You are already clean because of the word which I have spoken to you. Abide in Me, and I in you. As the branch cannot bear fruit of itself, unless it abides in the vine, neither can you, unless you abide in Me. I am the vine, you are the branches. He who abides in Me, and I in him, bears much fruit; for without Me you can do nothing (John 15:1-5, *NKJV*).

As was His custom, Jesus used an everyday illustration that His listeners would relate to almost immediately. His disciples—all reared in Jewish homes—knew well that Israel was pictured in the Old Testament as a vine or the vineyard of God.

Through the prophet Jeremiah, God reminds Israel she was planted "a noble vine, a seed of highest quality" (Jer. 2:21, *NKJV*).

When the psalmist sang of how God brought the Israelites out of slavery to Pharaoh, he said, "You have brought a vine out of Egypt; You have cast out the nations, and planted it. You prepared room for it, And caused it to take deep root, And it filled the land" (Ps. 80:8,9, *NKJV*).

One of the great glories of the temple at Jerusalem was a huge golden vine mounted on the front of the Holy Place. Devout Jews who could afford it were honored to give gold to mold a new bunch of grapes onto that vine. Jesus' disciples knew well that the vine played a key role in Jewish imagery, that it was the key symbol of the nation of Israel itself.[5]

But Jesus' disciples also knew that, while the vine was the symbol of Israel, it was also its mark of shame. The prophets had revealed in strong and condemning words that Israel had turned out to be an empty, degenerate vine (see Hos. 10:1; Jer. 2:21). When Jesus said, "I am the true vine," He was serving notice that He had come from God and that the way to a true relationship to God was through Him. True salvation is not found in being a Jew—part of the wayward fruitless vine—but in a living relationship to the Son of God.[6]

To have that living relationship, we are to "abide in Christ." What, exactly, does this mean? Contemporary dictionaries tell us that abiding involves being patient, persevering, accepting consequences, putting up with or tolerating.[7]

The New Testament word used for abide has a more intimate, personal meaning, which is brought out in modern translations:

Remain in Me (*NIV*);
Live in Me (*TLB*);
Dwell in Me (*NEB*).

J. B. Phillips says it best, perhaps, when he translates John 15:4,5 (italics mine):

> You can produce nothing unless you go on *growing* in me. I am the vine itself; you are the branches. It is the man who shares my life and whose life I share who proves fruitful. For apart from me you can do nothing at all.

As we have seen time and again in earlier chapters, the secret to Jesus' earthly ministry was His constant contact with His heavenly Father. The Son shared His life with the Father and the Father shared His life with the Son.

Because we put such strong emphasis on the deity of Christ, we sometimes forget that He was also completely human. He didn't automatically remain in or live in His heavenly Father; He had to maintain His own devotional life, just as you and I do. In William Barclay's words, "There must be no day when we never think of Jesus and feel His presence." Barclay goes on to say that constant contact with Christ means "arranging life, arranging prayer, arranging silence in such a way that there is never a day when we give ourselves a chance to forget Him."[8]

While working on this book, I read for the first time Andrew Murray's classic commentary on John 15, *Abide* in Christ. Following are a few brief excerpts from comments I wrote in my journal after each daily reading of Murray's thoughts:

———————

Why am I too busy?
1. Life throws curves.
2. I bite off too much.
3. I do not always use my time wisely.
What can I do? Andrew Murray says abide
in Christ.
But I am too busy.
Precisely.

When I abide in Christ I find rest. The pressure is on. The work piles up, but Jesus didn't say, "I'll take it away." Instead He said, "*In the work* I can give you rest—inner strength and peace."

Jesus is the "I" of my hurricane. He gives rest, not necessarily to my body or my brain but to my soul—when I surrender. But I am still prone to wander and fail to abide. I am a sheep...maybe a goat, and we know what happens to goats. Lord, please be my shepherd—I need some rest!

According to Murray, the highway to holiness is downhill, if you stay on the road. If I am not as holy as God would like, it is because I'm allowing certain shoots of my old nature to pop out and bear the old fruit. I need to ask God to "prune those little suckers"—every day.

Lord, I seem to be writing something about which I know so little. On the other hand, I know a lot about the problem. For example, how can I abide and concentrate on everything I have to do, too? Murray says God is there even when I'm concentrating on the business at hand. Abiding doesn't demand that I be constantly aware I'm abiding!

According to Murray, abiding is like gathering manna. The Israelites could only gather enough for each day, and they had to gather early before the rush. In the same way we abide in Christ a day at a time. In Murray's words, "Our daily life becomes a wonderful interchange of God's daily grace and our daily praise."[9]

Today's reading advises procrastinators to start abiding now, no matter how you feel. You don't grow to a certain point where you can abide. Abiding comes first, growth afterwards.

There is no more important lesson for any abider than developing stillness of the soul. The more silent you are, the louder the Spirit will speak.

No matter how fouled up and fragmented I get, Jesus loves me with a gentle, tender love. As Murray puts it, "With patience inconceivable, He bears with our slowness."[10] If only deadlines and publishers felt the same way!

There are days when the writing comes into full focus, for just a brief instant. Then the enormity of the task seems to wipe everything out. But I must press on through the tunnel. What if there is no light at the end? But do I really need one? Can't faith light the way? (See Ps. 119:105.)

As I look over these journal entries, I realize that coping in the fast lane is not a matter of "letting go and letting God." Instead:

LET GO TO LET GOD IN

Let God into your life all the way. Allow Him to direct you as you decide your goals, priorities and plans, rather than asking Him to be a consultant *after* you have made all your own decisions.

God does not want to be on the periphery of your life. He is not waiting out there shrouded in the mists, letting you ignore Him. Instead, He is knocking at your heart's door, asking you to let Him in. In Revelation 3:20, Jesus says, "Behold, I stand at the door and knock. If anyone hears My voice and opens the door, I will come in" (NKJV). This verse is often quoted out of context for evangelistic purposes, but it was really written to Christians for another reason.

In his fine little book, *Time for All Things,* Charlie Shedd tells of a youth group that was meditating one morning on Revelation 3:20. Suddenly one of the girls in the group made an exciting discovery: "I get it! Prayer isn't my asking God. It's Him asking me. What it means is, I don't need to beat on His door. He's already knocking on mine."[11]

Shedd speculates that Revelation 3:20 might be the best scriptural definition of perfect prayer. And then he adds:

> Grand new vistas come to the student of spiritual living when he understands that prayer's first act is not on the human side. The initial move of real prayer is from God. Banging at the gates of heaven in frantic appeal is prayer, of a sort. But prayer of the finer sort is hearing the knock of Him Who is nearer to us than breathing—closer than hands and feet.[12]

If we are to have time for everything we have to do, we must first give Christ every one of these things each day. Invite Christ into your center, and you will find yourself in His. The fast pace, the busy-ness, the hassle and stress may surround you, but it no longer has the same impact. You have slowed down to catch up with God. And you know that your time and your life are safe in His hands.

Lord, sometimes I still have to hurry, but, please, never stop slowing me down.

Re-read this chapter (and possibly other chapters) and then make a short list of exactly how you plan to "let go to let God in." Formulate your personal strategy for "abiding in Christ."

Notes

1. See especially Alan Laekin, *How to Get Control of Your Time and Your Life* (New York: Peter H. Wyden, Inc., 1973). Also available in Signet paperback edition, 1974.
2. Henri J. M. Nouwen, *Making All Things New* (San Francisco: Harper and Row Publishers, 1981), p. 25.
3. William P. Clemmons, *Discovering the Depths* (Nashville: Broadman Press, 1976), p. 41.
4. Ibid., p. 21.
5. See William Barclay, *The Daily Study Bible, The Gospel of John*, Vol. 2 (Edinburgh: The St. Andrew Press, 1955), p. 201.
6. Ibid., p. 202.
7. See William Morris, Editor, *The American Heritage Dictionary of the English Language* (New York: American Heritage Publishing Company; Boston: Houghton Mifflin Company, 1969), p. 3.
8. See William Barclay, *The Gospel of John*, p. 205.
9. Andrew Murray, *Abide in Christ* (Grand Rapids, MI: Zondervan Publishing House).
10. Andrew Murray, *Abide in Christ.*
11. Charlie Shedd, *Time for All Things* (Nashville: Abingdon Press, 1962), p. 37.
12. Ibid., p. 37.